FRIENDS & LOVERS:

How to Meet the People You Want to Meet

Steve Bhaerman & Don McMillan

Writer's Digest Books

Cincinnati, Ohio

Friends & Lovers: How to Meet the People You Want to Meet. Copyright © 1986 by Steve Bhaerman and Don McMillan. Printed and bound in the United States of America. All rights reserved. No part of this book may be reproduced in any form or by any electronic or mechanical means, including information storage and retrieval systems, without permission in writing from the publisher, except by a reviewer, who may quote brief passages in a review. Published by Writer's Digest Books, an imprint of F&W Publications Inc., 1507 Dana Avenue, Cincinnati, Ohio 45207. First edition.

Bhaerman, Steve.
    Friends and lovers.
    Includes index.
    1. Single people—United States. 2. Interpersonal relations. 3. Dating (Social customs) 4. Mate selection—United States. I. McMillan, Don, 1943- II. Title.
HQ800.4.U6B43   1986   646.7'7   85-29422
ISBN 0-89879-161-8

Design by Joan Ann Jacobus

92 91 90 89   7 6 5 4 3

Contents

Introduction

Some people have all the luck when it comes to meeting the right people. Or so it seems. You know the ones we're talking about: those lucky individuals who seem to have the knack for effortlessly meeting and getting to know the people they want to meet. They're not necessarily smarter or more beautiful than the rest of us, but they seem to have something that draws others to them like a magnet.

It's true, some of us do have the ability to meet others naturally. The good news is, this is no accident of birth but a skill that you too can learn. The purpose of this book is to help you acquire that all-important skill, first by helping you find and create your ideal people-meeting environment, and then by letting you know how others successfully make contact, build rapport, and form lasting friendships and relationships.

If you've been feeling out of your element in situations supposedly designed for meeting other people, you're not alone. A large majority of the people we interviewed for this book felt the same way. Many of them suffered through less-than-wonderful people-meeting situations before they realized that it's difficult to find the right person in the wrong place. How do you find that right place? The fun social activities you love are the key to finding the right place—and the right people. So anytime you feel out of place in a social situation, you know that a key ingredient is missing. And that ingredient is your kind of fun activity.

In the hundreds of interviews we've done, in our own personal experience, and in the seminars we've led on how to meet people, one theme came up over and over again. The times we meet and get to know new friends most easily and enjoyably are naturally those times we are engaged in the activities we love. Of course, there are exceptions. All of us know people who met and became close during power blackouts, in hospitals—even at funerals. It's possible to meet someone through friends and neighbors, at work or at school, and yes, at singles' bars. But if these settings haven't worked well for you, perhaps you need to make fun an integral part of your people-meeting plan.

If the idea of planning how you're going to meet people

seems too cold and calculating, consider the alternatives: doing the same old things that haven't worked, or leaving it to chance. You probably thought very carefully before accepting the job you now have; you prepared a résumé to reflect who you are and what you're looking for. You spent many hours researching job openings, and you probably examined the company as thoroughly as they examined you. All of this preparing, planning, and strategizing seems quite natural when it comes to our careers, but we sometimes forget that we can use these same skills to select and meet the people we want to meet.

It isn't that our social life is less important than our work life; some studies say it's *more* important. Researchers at the University of California at Berkeley found that people without spouses or friends had a death rate more than twice as high as those with social ties. This held true for both sexes and for all age groups and social classes and seemed to have little connection with other lifestyle factors such as drinking, smoking, or stress. The more such social ties, the lower the death rate.

Another Berkeley study of 3,000 Japanese-American men found that those who retained strong ties to the Japanese community showed a markedly lower incidence of heart disease, even when they smoked, drank, and were under stress. On the other hand, those men who had little or no connection to the community had five times as much heart disease. Researchers could only conclude that close social ties made the difference.

But meeting people is far more than a human need—it is a lifetime adventure. If you look back over your life, you'll notice that the best times you've had were times you shared with other people. Take a few moments right now to think about some of those great times and persons who've enriched your life. Just as those you have met have shaped who you are, so the people you have yet to meet will have a profound impact on your future. In light of this, don't you think that actively pursuing a social plan is at least as important as career planning?

If the people in our lives are so important to us, why do we so often leave meetings to chance, fate, and others' ideas of what we "ought to do" to meet people? For one thing, most of us grew up believing that we meet others "naturally." And most of us did—through our families, on our block, at church or school. When we were in high school, and even college, an entire community of our peers was available to us daily. But now that we are adults in a highly mobile society, our workplace and communities may not provide this ready-made pool of potential friends. Many forget this and passively wait for the right people to come along. Or, they haunt the singles' bars, hoping the right person will cross their paths there—even though they sense they don't have a ghost of a chance.

People are often reluctant to actively plan how they will meet others because having a plan seems to directly contradict the romantic notion of the "magical meeting" with an exotic stranger. Let us assure you that designing and planning doesn't destroy the magic, but actually increases the chances of it occurring with the right person. By looking in the right places, you're most likely to find the ones who'll be magic for *you*—those likely to like you for who you are.

The principles we spell out in this book are simple, but often overlooked as you search for friends and lovers in settings that may be right for others, but are wrong for you. If you have the sense that you are the right person in the wrong milieu, you'll find this book a friendly guide for doing the things you love to do with the individuals you'd like to meet, and helping you create a network of friends—and maybe even for finding a life mate. We can't guarantee magic, but we can help you increase the possibility that magic will happen simply by shifting the emphasis from pressure to fun. This book will also help you:

- Zero in on your favorite social activities and turn them into enjoyable ways to meet the right people.
- Identify those you want to meet so you'll know them when you meet them.
- Discover and select the right people-meeting settings for you.
- "Grow your own fun" instead of waiting for it to come to you.
- Prepare for having fun by having fun preparing.
- Feel comfortable and confident in new social situations.
- Establish rapport easily, ask for future contact comfortably, and if necessary, exit gracefully.
- Use fun activities to turn acquaintances into friends.

HOW THIS BOOK CAME ABOUT

This book grew out of the exasperation so many of the people we knew felt about meeting the people *they* wanted to meet.

As one woman (let's call her Janet) put it, "I'm reasonably attractive, friendly, intelligent. Most things in my life seem to be working well. But each weekend, I set out to do things to meet people and I always come home frustrated. I think I'm going to the places where single people meet, but I just never seem to get noticed there. Or if I do get noticed, it's the wrong kind of attention. I feel defensive about talking to complete strangers, because you never know who they might be. And I keep getting the feeling, is there something wrong with me?"

We heard many others express similar feelings, using words like "uncomfortable," "superficial," "unsatisfying," even "dehumanizing," to describe the singles' scene they were accustomed to. Like Janet, most of these people were otherwise happy and successful, yet they felt they lacked some mysterious ability that would make it easier for them to meet others in these settings.

Numerous books have been written on how to pick up men and women, how to read body language, how to look available (or unavailable), how to dress, impress, intimidate, seduce. As far as we were concerned, there was ample information for those who wanted to get better at playing the singles' game. But we noticed that very little had been written about how to find and create settings that allow you to meet people comfortably and enjoyably, where you can be yourself and get to know others at your own rate and pace, where you can meet people who are likely to like you for who you really are. And that was the book we set out to write.

We began by asking people we knew to describe the times when it was easiest and most enjoyable for them to meet people *and* they were able to meet the people they wanted to meet. We also asked ourselves the same question. The one common denominator we found time and again was fun, specifically a fun social activity that we shared with others. The activity itself didn't matter. It could have involved sports, artistic pursuits, music, dancing, lectures, classes, anything from skydiving to bird watching, as long as it was truly fun and involved others.

We continued our interviews and heard more and more stories of how people met the significant persons in their lives through fun activity. And in our seminars and classes, we began to teach others how to identify what they love to do and where to go to pursue those activities in a social setting. But this raised another important issue. "I'm already doing those activities," we were sometimes told. "But I just can't seem to make contact with others." So we asked ourselves two more questions: What did those people who made contact easily do that the rest of us didn't do? And what were we doing right when we *did* establish rapport? Once again, we interviewed people to find out what exactly they did that worked and didn't work. The success patterns and pitfalls we uncovered in these interviews enabled us to write the sections on preparation, making contact, establishing rapport, and turning acquaintances into friends.

The suggestions we offer throughout the book are based directly on the interviews we did, as are the stories we use as examples. We sometimes changed a few of the details to disguise the identities of the storytellers, and several times we created composites out of two or more stories. However, all of the stories accurately reflect the experiences of those we interviewed and those who participated in our seminars and classes.

Keep in mind that the things that worked for others are presented not so much as formulas for you to blindly follow as options for you to try out and to adjust to your own personality and situation. As you combine your own past success patterns with the many options that have worked for others, you will find yourself feeling more comfortable and confident meeting the people you want to meet. Best of all, you will be having fun meeting them.

HOW TO GET THE MOST OUT OF THIS BOOK

We have designed this book in such a way that it will be easy for you to try these ideas out. Of course, no book can work unless you the reader are willing to make it work. Words are just words; to get results, actions are required. Here are some suggestions for how to become an active user of this book:

1. BRING THIS BOOK TO LIFE—INTERACT WITH IT! Writing has sometimes been likened to creating a child; an entirely new entity has been brought forth with the potential to act on and influence the world. But unlike the human baby who grasps and crawls and moves out to explore life, the book remains dormant until it is picked up, read, digested, and acted upon. In a sense, the book is Sleeping Beauty and only you the reader, Prince (or Princess) Charming, can bring it to life.

2. READ THE BOOK ACTIVELY, NOT PASSIVELY. Read with a questioning yet open mind. Take notes. Underline passages that particularly apply to you. Agree or disagree emphatically in the margins. Select and use what is useful for you.

3. USE THE BOOK TO EXAMINE YOURSELF. Take the time to answer the questions in each chapter, to do the various exercises, and to evaluate your progress. Conscious change comes about from self-knowledge. Use the questions in the book to become clearer about where you are, where you want to be, and what it's going to take to get there.

4. TRY THE IDEAS OUT IN YOUR LIFE. Socrates said, "The unexamined life is not worth living." Well, it's also true that the unlived life is not worth examining. If you don't take these ideas out of the realm of thought and into the arena of action, you will have nothing to evaluate. Be an experimenter. Test the ideas so that you create a people-meeting approach that works for you.

5. PLAY THE BELIEVING GAME. In his book, *Writing Without Teachers,* Peter Elbow compares what he calls the doubting game and the believing game. The doubting game is at its best healthy skepticism that demands to be shown proof. Often, however, we approach new situations with only a critical eye, eager to pounce on these new ideas and prove them wrong. To most effectively evaluate new ideas, you must try them on as you would a pair of shoes. One man we spoke with said he owed his success in meeting people specifically to trying out behaviors he wouldn't have dreamed of trying otherwise. The things that worked for him, he stayed with; those that didn't, he discarded. But he had no way of knowing which was which until he tried them out. If you're skeptical of one of our approaches, see what happens if you try it anyway.

6. KEEP A PEOPLE-MEETING NOTEBOOK. A notebook or journal is an excellent tool for recording progress, keeping yourself on track, and "talking to yourself." It is essentially a place to set down the results of your experiments. It is a place to jot down useful insights, quotations, feedback from others in your life, a place to test your ability to observe others, and a means of becoming a better listener to yourself. Writing is a great way to appreciate solitude, and a way to clarify your thoughts. As E.M. Forster said, "How can I know what I think until I hear what I say?"

7. WRITE US! One of the advantages of writing a book is that you get to talk at length without being interrupted. On the other hand, you have no way to be sure if anyone is listening, no way to gauge the impact the book is having. That's why we invite written comment. Tell us what has worked for you, what hasn't, what we need to emphasize more, what is superfluous. Is there anything we haven't included? Do you have an anecdote that illustrates a point we have made—or disputes it? In your application of this material, you are in a sense a co-author of this book. Let us know what you have created with this information.

8. GET A FRIEND INVOLVED. One way to make reading the book and using the suggestions easier and more fun is to do it with a friend. Having a buddy to check in with and share your adventures with will help keep you active and on track. He or she can help you brainstorm new people-meeting situations, shore up your courage by going with you into new settings, offer support and encouragement when you're stuck or discouraged. Your comrade will be an excellent source of ideas, activities, and of course, potential friends—particularly if he or she shares many of your interests.

9. MAKE PROGRESS AT YOUR OWN RATE AND PACE. This book is designed so that you can pick out the ideas that are most suitable for you and bring them into your life as quickly—or as slowly—as you like. If you find that you're comparing yourself unfavorably with others, or are discouraged about your rate of progress, remember that no skill is really learned in one try. Think of how you learned how to walk, ride a bicycle, or drive a car. It took time and practice before you were able to do it unconsciously. As you apply your most resourceful and capable self to practicing these skills in your life, you will notice that you are getting better at it day by day. And before you know it, you will have developed a lifelong skill that is as automatic for you as driving a car, riding a bike, or walking down the street.

10. ABOVE ALL, HAVE FUN. As we talk to people about how they've met others in the past, we find again and again that meeting people is simply a by-product of having fun. If you haven't been able to make meeting people work, make it play! Look at every people-meeting situation as an exciting adventure—

because it is. There's no scarcity of terrific people. And there are as many ways to have fun as there are people to meet. The people you want to meet are out there doing the things you love to do; this book will help you find them. We wish you good luck in using this information—and great times!

Steve Bhaerman
Don McMillan

Ann Arbor, Michigan
October, 1985

Chapter 1

66 Why what you've been doing hasn't worked 99

It's Friday night. After a long week of work, you have come home, relaxed, showered, and put on your best clothes. Maybe tonight you'll meet that special person—or at least someone whose company you enjoy. Getting ready, you're filled with excitement and expectation. You try to forget all the other times you have gone to meet people and it didn't work. Maybe this time things will be different.

As you walk into the room full of strangers, suddenly your mood changes to one of fear and apprehension. You envy the others who sit or stand talking in clusters. You imagine approaching someone who catches your eye, but the prospect of walking up to a total stranger leaves your mouth dry and your palms wet. You feel immobilized. As you retreat to the small group of people you already know, you wonder, "Is there something wrong with me?"

Maybe—particularly if you're a woman—you are approached, but the attention is anything but welcome. You feel like a prize fish the man will brag to his buddies about on Monday—after he's given you his line and reeled you in. If you're a guy, you might fantasize about dancing with the woman you see across the room, but your fantasy turns sour as you imagine all of the unpleasant ways she can say no. So you clutch your drink tighter, strike an impressive pose and let this one go by. You generalize. You stereotype. "These women are stuck up." "These men are only after one thing." You go home bitter and disappointed.

Perhaps you've gone beyond the bar scene and joined a singles' group. Here at least you'll get a chance to get to know people over a period of time. You're surprised to find that a lot of people in this group are "collectors" who seem to be frightened of relating beyond sex. The parties are all the same; you don't find the people particularly interesting, but what else can you do? You go back week after week, hoping it will get better, but it never does.

Or maybe a friend at work notices your dilemma and offers to fix you up with someone who'd be just perfect for you. "Jeff is a really neat guy. I know you two will hit it off." "Jeanine is a knockout. Wait'll you see her." All week long you indulge in anticipation and fantasy. This person—whom you haven't even met yet—might be the one who will change your life. The night finally arrives, you go forth in the innocence of hope—and you are disappointed. Jeff is a chainsmoker, and you hate smoke. "Hey, I'm in no hurry," he says to you over dinner. "Don't feel like you have to go to bed with me immediately. After all, we've got all night."

Jeanine is attractive all right, but clearly not your type. You were looking forward to a light dinner followed by a stroll in the park. Jeanine is hardly able to stand—let alone walk—in her spike heels. You figured you'd go out dancing later in the evening. She doesn't dance. Instead, she suggests an expensive restaurant. Reluctantly, you agree. After all, this is a date, right? Once inside, Jeanine is in her element. She orders the most expensive food, wine, and dessert. The evening ends, you find yourself out $80—and you didn't even have fun.

Exaggerations? Not really. Yes, there are people who regularly and easily meet people in singles' bars. Yes, there are some excellent singles' organizations where people have fun with people who enjoy similar activities. Yes, there are couples who met on a blind date and are still together. Nevertheless, most people have little success with these traditional methods of meeting people. Worse than that, they often blame themselves, the other people, or the situation for their difficulty instead of finding methods that can work. Many attractive and otherwise competent people feel so frustrated about meeting people that they give up completely and resign themselves to being alone. One woman put it poignantly when she said, "The TV is my lover."

If you have found "tried and true" methods of meeting people trying and truly frustrating, it's not because there is something wrong with you, the other person, or even the situation. Each of us already has within us the ability and potential to successfully meet the people we want to meet. This book is about discovering what your resources are—and turning your unpleasant experiences into comfortable, easy, enjoyable ways of meeting the people you want to meet.

When we asked people what they imagined their ideal people-meeting situations to be like, the first word that came up was "comfortable." They wanted to get to know people gradually, at their own pace. They also wanted to be sure that the people they were meeting were the kinds of people they wanted to be with. They wanted to feel as if they were in their element. And they wanted to have fun. Keeping this in mind, it's not difficult to see why many of the things we normally do to meet people lead to failure and frustration. The methods that don't work have some things in common:

1. TOO MUCH PRESSURE Both men and women who have tried the bar scene complain that they're being looked over, and that it's extremely difficult to walk up to someone and make contact. Says Lisa, a thirty-five-year-old nurse, "I don't like the looks you get when you walk in. You are sort of looked up and down, undressed by the men sitting at the bar. If I go to a bar with some women friends to get something to eat, I'm very careful to sit away from the action so I don't send any signals that I want to be approached."

Marge, thirty-two years old and recently remarried, says, "When I was in college and I walked into the local college bar, I knew a lot of people. Back then, the bar was a place to hang out and meet your friends. After my divorce, I tried going to bars and I hated the whole game of waiting until someone approached you. The only women who seemed to do all right in that scene were the ones who looked like they were right out of the pages of *Cosmopolitan*."

Not surprisingly, men, too, feel threatened and pressured with the bar scene. Says Dave, a thirty-eight-year-old computer designer, "It's just too difficult to walk up to a complete stranger and make conversation or ask her to dance. I feel absolutely stuck in those types of situations."

Greg is a thirty-year-old parks employee and part-time student. He has an outgoing, animated personality and has been involved with theater since his college days. In spite of his experience as an actor, Greg has had little luck meeting women in bars. "I hate the bar scene," he says. "I've never been successful there. What I usually end up doing is getting two or three barstools away from some woman I'm attracted to, drinking a pitcher of beer and going home. I'm uncomfortable in that atmosphere. The things that come naturally to me aren't there."

2. TOO SUPERFICIAL   Part of the frustration that Lisa, Marge, Dave, and Greg feel about singles' bars is that your first attempt tends to be your only one. In choosing people to approach or deciding whom you are going to respond to, all you have to go on initially is physical appearance, which may not reveal much about personality, interests, or whether this person would be suitable in other ways. Women particularly have trouble when they go to singles' bars because their intentions may be quite different from the men they are likely to meet. Says Marge, "I used to go to bars looking for someone to date, but I eventually gave up on that expectation. Those kinds of bars are primarily a meat-market."

Melissa, a thirty-three-year-old woman, gave up on singles' bars because, "Any time I became friendly or asked a guy to dance, he would assume I wanted to go to bed with him."

3. NO WAY TO KNOW WHO IS SUITABLE   In a crowded bar or party scene, there may be someone in the room who could become a good friend or companion, but how would you know? Either you must take the chance of walking up to that person and introducing yourself, you wait for the stranger to come to you, or you wait for an introduction. Likewise, when someone "fixes you up," you really have no way of knowing beforehand whether he or she will be suitable. Says Marge, "People think they know your type when they really have no idea what your type is. The fact that someone else did the choosing takes a lot of the fun and spontaneity out of it right away. After several experiences of feeling trapped with someone I wouldn't have chosen, I gave up on being fixed up by anybody."

4. IT DOESN'T FEEL RIGHT FOR YOU   Although many people feel at home in a party atmosphere, there are those who prefer smaller groups. Janet, a twenty-five-year-old woman, says, "When I first started going to a singles' group after college, I noticed that people who already knew each other would tend to stay together. Me, I would freeze up and feel self-conscious. I just don't like gatherings where there are more than twenty people. It took me a while to realize it, but large groups are just not for me."

Says Roger, a forty-two-year-old attorney, "I once went to one of those singles' groups where they discuss books or have a lecture and I had a terrible time. There wasn't enough interaction. I was so bored, I never returned." Roger's passions include sailing and racquetball, so this activity didn't work for him. For others, however, the discussion groups might have been a lot of fun.

Chuck, a thirty-one-year-old psychologist, decided to take disco dancing lessons a few years ago. "I thought this would be an excellent way to meet women," he says. "At first, I enjoyed it; there was a party every Friday night after class. Yet, I never fit in with this group, and I had trouble relating to the instructors—they all seemed so in love with themselves. I remember one beautiful female instructor looking depressed one day. When I asked what was wrong, she told me she'd spent the whole afternoon at the mall and hadn't found a dress that she liked. This reflected the depth of the people in the group—needless to say I decided not to sign up for the class again."

5. TOO MUCH EMPHASIS ON MEETING PEOPLE, NOT ENOUGH ON HAVING FUN One of the biggest problems with situations designed for people to meet is that the very emphasis on meeting people gets in the way of having fun. People become self-conscious as they size one another up. They frown instead of smile, or if they do smile it's not genuine. Roger says, "Most of the singles' groups I've been to feel contrived. It's like contact is being forced. That's no fun."

Says Chuck, "One of the most important things I learned about meeting women was to forget the 'sex connection' and just enjoy myself, taking the time to talk and really get to know the women I encountered. I developed a more carefree attitude that way." And Michael, a thirty-eight-year-old advertising executive, says, "Whenever I feel stuck about not being able to meet the people I want to meet, I stop whatever I'm doing and remind myself to have fun. This usually gets me back on track."

One of the biggest mistakes you can make is setting out to meet the "right person" instead of just enjoying yourself. You're adding more pressure to an already pressurized situation. Your good time becomes dependent on who walks in the door rather than on your own ability to have fun. And you set yourself up for almost certain disappointment. Says Janice, a twenty-six-year-old receptionist, "I used to come home from an evening at the bar feeling like a failure when I didn't find someone to go out with. At some point, I decided to give up on meeting people and just enjoy the dancing. Now, whether I meet new people or not, if I have a great time dancing I look at the evening as a success."

Like Janice, the people we spoke with who were able to turn their people-meeting frustration into success were those who turned their attention away from high-pressure, high-risk people-meeting situations, and instead began spending more time having fun, doing what they love to do—with others. In the next chapter you'll learn exactly how they do it.

Chapter 2

"The best way to meet people is to do what you love to do"

In our research, our seminars, and in our own experience, we have found that those who are most successful at meeting people—and those who enjoy the people-meeting process most—use some very specific strategies. They aren't always conscious of using these strategies, but they use them nonetheless. Each of these strategies is a key that will open your life to more of the people you want to meet. Throughout the book, these keys will be highlighted so you can build your own action plan for success.

Of all the many keys we will be presenting, there is one "master key," that when applied will bring a whole world of fun and new people into your life. This key may seem simple, but we assure you, it is central if you want to be more comfortable and have more fun meeting people. Here it is:

KEY 1

> "When you are actively doing
> the things you enjoy,
> having fun with others,
> and thus being yourself,
> you meet the people
> you want to meet naturally."

There's something about having fun that creates and enhances the chemistry between people. Whether you're like the woman who told us she met her current boyfriend when they both were frogs at a Halloween party, or the attorney who first met his current business partner on the tennis court, when you are absorbed in an activity you love there's no room for feeling self-conscious or self-critical. You're having so much fun that you can't help radiating confidence, enthusiasm, joy for life—and attractiveness.

JoAnne, a forty-three-year-old real estate broker, still gets goose bumps thinking about a ski trip she went on two years ago. "It was challenging and adventurous to live a little dangerously. I really enjoyed building the new skill and becoming more graceful each time. This sense of accomplishment did wonders for my self-esteem. Afterwards, it was easy to meet people at the ski lodge. Everyone was physically exhausted, yet flushed with the excitement of skiing all day. They seemed eager to hear about particularly exciting runs or funny crashes. Later on, we spent time in the large hot tub, but it was more difficult to meet people there, with everyone feeling exposed and vulnerable in their bathing suits. I found the best time to meet people was when I just finished a run, or was reliving it at the bar. I made a bunch of friends whom I continued to enjoy for a long time afterwards."

Marie, who by her own admission has been hooked on movies since she was twelve, was feeling isolated after moving to a new town. She missed having friends to go to the movies with, and wondered if there was a way she could meet people through that interest. She told us: "After I read about a cinema society in our town, I called them up, met some of the people involved, and I've been working with them ever since. Several months ago, we invited a famous director to a showing of his latest film and had a reception afterward. Throughout the reception, I kept bumping into people who asked me everything from 'Where's the bathroom?' to 'How can I become a member of the cinema society?' Since then, I've seen some of those people elsewhere and gotten to know them better. One of the people I spoke to that night is a guy who shares my passion for the movies. We disagree about nearly every movie we see, and that makes for lively discussions. But we seem to agree in a lot of other ways, and we've become quite close."

Instead of passively waiting around for "Mr. Right," JoAnne and Marie took charge of their own situations. They decided to go out and have fun, and as a natural result they met new people they liked. Contrast the exhilaration of a ski weekend or the excitement of meeting your favorite film director with the pressure and anxiety of a situation specifically designed for meeting people. What did JoAnne conclude about her experience? "As soon as I found that I could actually meet people and have fun at the same time, I immediately dropped the social activities in my life that were not fun. I figure, if I'm having a great time, even if I don't meet someone, I'm still ahead."

KEY 2

> " When you are enjoying yourself, the signal you seem to be sending is, 'Having a wonderful time, wish you were here.' "

What people do you find most attractive? Imagine entering a room full of men and women. Who are you naturally drawn to? Are there some people who seem to stand out from the crowd? You look at them and you say to yourself, "Well, it isn't their beauty, at least not in the Hollywood sense. And it isn't necessarily the clothes they are wearing. It's just that they have a certain glow." That glow these attractive people are emanating is the glow of being totally alive in the present moment and enjoying themselves.

"One of the best times I've ever had was when our softball team was so bad that we lost every game," says Bill, an executive with a computer firm. "We decided to give awards for the worst plays, the most most dramatic misses, the best form on a total mess-up. We gave the awards at a bar, and most of the other teams were jealous of our camaraderie and the sheer fun we were having. I think I must have made at least 1000 toasts to the best of the worst. We even had T-shirts printed up for award-winners. That's proba-bly the best time I've had with a group of people, and I think it was because we kept the focus on fun without competitiveness and criti-cism. I still keep in contact with these people and they maintain that theirs is the most popular team to be on and their post-game parties are the most fun. They have gone on to organize ski trips in the win-ter, and as many as two hundred people have shown up because they know it'll be a great time."

Says Janet, twenty-five: "One of the best times I had re-cently was when a group of friends and I went to a local comedy club. One of my friends was laughing so hard that the people at the next table started to smile at us, and in between acts we struck up a conversation. After the show, it seemed natural for us to join forces and go out for a late snack. One of the guys in the other group sug-gested having a comedy potluck where everyone brings a dish and their favorite comedy record or tape. We all got very excited about the idea, and I'm looking forward to getting to know these people better."

Look on any list of desired traits for a friend or spouse, and you'll see "sense of humor" up there near the top of the list. Hu-mor, provided it is not hostile, can be an excellent way to connect with another person. In Victor Borge's words, "Laughter is the shortest distance between two people." It was Janet's friend's sense of humor that "broke the ice" and gave the people at the other table an excuse to start a conversation.

Whatever it is that we love to do, being totally absorbed in that activity ties up the mental circuits we use to criticize our-selves. (This is particularly true if we are being silly!) We are unself-conscious; we are too busy having fun to care about whether our hair is correct, our outfit coordinates, or whether something stupid is about to come out of our mouths. It is this active behavior, not merely physical appearance, that makes us truly attractive. A friend of ours was going through his high school yearbook looking for the picture of the girl he remembered as being most attractive. The pho-to he located turned out to be of a rather pleasant looking but plain young woman. Nevertheless, he insisted she was the most attrac-tive, and his face lit up as he described her. "She had a way of mak-ing everything fun," he said, "and she had this mischievous smile. She always seemed to be creating theme parties and starting crazy trends, and she always had people flocking around her."

That's why Bill's inept softball team attracted so many fans. When we see people who are already enjoying themselves without us, we feel attracted to them. (Perhaps by hanging around that person, some of the glow will reflect on us?) All of us have experienced being in the presence of a lively person—we leave feeling joyful, energized, excited about life. Those are the traits we seek in others.

KEY 3

"Doing what you truly enjoy tells others who you truly are."

Much of the discomfort we associate with meeting other people stems from the mistaken belief that we have to be something other than ourselves for others to like us. We are constantly bombarded with advertisements that insist we need to look a certain way, dress a certain way, or use a particular deodorant or toothpaste in order to be attractive to others. While many of us laugh off these ads and claim that we're too sophisticated to be susceptible, these images tend to remind us of our imperfections. This is particularly true when we are not absorbed in activity, but are doing something that is specifically designed for meeting people. Then conversation tends to be superficial, focusing on what they do for a living, where they live, how old they are. Vital statistics are substituted for vital living in the moment, and what we get is a shopping list, not real people. In this context, we get to categorize a man as a lawyer, a salesman, a yuppie, a jock, yet we rarely get to know him for who he really is.

One evening, Marge decided to go to a weekly singles' group where they had a lecture, then a discussion. Because she arrived late, she had to wait a few minutes before being let in and found herself in a group of three men. One of the three seemed a bit shy and withdrawn and she decided to try to draw him out. He told her his name was George and she asked him what he did.

"I'm a financial analyst," he answered in a monotone.

"Do you enjoy it?"

"Not very much," he replied.

She was about to move on, when she decided to ask one more question. "Well," she asked, "what really turns you on?"

He lit up. "Sailing!" he said, and launched into an animated description of his last trip out on his boat and what he loved about it. She found his ON button as he began to relive his enjoyment of this activity. Even though she had never been sailing in her life, his enthusiasm drew her in. They made a date for the next night, and the next. And this sparked the beginning of a long relationship.

By getting George to talk about what he really loved to do, Marge was eventually able to find out who he was. This is especially true when people actually see us engaged in our favorite activities. Bob was painfully shy from the time he was a young child until he was past high school. Since he enjoyed music, Bob began to sing and play guitar for his own pleasure. After a while, he found that music could be a bridge between himself and other people. "Even though I was still basically shy and unsure of myself," he says, "when people began telling me how much they enjoyed hearing my music, I came out of my shell a little more. Not only did I have the intrinsic pleasure the music gave me, but I also felt valued as a person. Since then, music has enabled me to make countless friends, and I've even gotten some consulting jobs just because someone heard me play."

Bob used what he enjoyed doing as a vehicle to take him from shyness to involvement with others. Doing what you love to do and sharing this activity with others is "truth in advertising" because it gives others a true and favorable picture of who you are and what they are likely to enjoy about you. The more clearly you show others what turns you on the more likely you are to attract people who will be attracted to YOU.

KEY 4

"Where are the people you'd like to meet? They're doing the things you like to do!"

Studies show that one of the key components of a successful relationship is shared activities. The person who loves to spend all winter outdoors will never get past the initial attraction to the movie buff, unless the two find some things they both enjoy doing. When we put ourselves in a situation where there are others who enjoy the same activities, we increase the chances of forming a lasting bond.

Shortly after her divorce, Elaine, twenty-four, took a job working at a racquetball court. "I took the job because I enjoyed racquetball," she says, "and I had lots of opportunities to play. I picked up a lot of games and met a lot of new people just because I loved to play racquetball. Again, my intention was not to meet new people necessarily, but it worked out that way, because there were always people who had to talk to me. When I did take the first step, it was easy. If I asked some people to play and they turned me down, I didn't take it personally. It just meant that they didn't want to play. I played a lot of racquetball and met a number of men I went out with. Once while I was behind the counter, I began talking with an attractive guy about racquetball. We played together, started going out, and ended up getting married."

Elaine put herself in a situation where she naturally would meet people who enjoyed the same activities. She was in her element, and meeting suitable people was effortless.

Janet was having trouble meeting the kind of people she wanted to meet. "I've always felt intimidated by bars," she says. "I sort of assume no one is going to talk to me and I shrink into a corner. For a while, I tried being part of a campus religious group. We had fun, but I never really felt these were my kind of people. Recently I told a friend that I really enjoyed singing. He introduced me to his roommate, who played guitar. I went to a party over there, we started singing and had a great time. There were about a dozen people there, a number of whom I hadn't met. Since then, we've made plans to get together and have more singing parties."

When you share activities you love, you are more likely to meet people who share your values as well. A number of people we spoke with said they enjoy attending personal growth workshops. Says Jim, "One of the added benefits of going to these workshops is that I find it's very easy to meet people there who value self-development. Otherwise, they wouldn't be there."

Once you have found people who share your basic values through shared activities, they in turn will introduce you to their friends. As Bill, the softball player, told us, once he found a group of people who enjoyed playing softball without being overly concerned about winning, he became friends of their friends and so on, until he had a well-developed social network. The more clearly you

identify what it is that YOU really love to do, the more likely you are
to identify people out there who enjoy those things as well.

KEY 5

" Activity is the most natural and comfortable way to make contact. "

Judy, a single woman of thirty, recalls, "I was at this folk
dance camp in West Virginia where there were about 250 people of
all ages, styles, and sizes. I met this one guy right away on Friday
night during a line dance. We just started talking and we hit it off. It
wasn't that he was incredibly cute, but he was a superb dancer. The
theme of this particular evening was the Fifties, and he taught me
how to jitterbug. We enjoyed the weekend together and even
though we lived in different states, we traveled to see one another."
Judy concluded that the best way for her to meet people was without trying. "Just go out and enjoy yourself with other people."

Across a crowded room, in a classroom, in a work setting, Judy might never have spoken with this young man. But on the
dance floor it was a different story. When you are enjoying yourself
with another person doing an activity you both like, your interests
form a bridge for future friendship. You are motivated to get to
know each other; there is a natural connection. Automatically you
know that you have a lot in common. There's no need to explain
yourself, present yourself, or run down a list of your qualifications.
You get to see, hear, feel, and know another person without either of
you filling out a survey form.

Sometimes a bond is created without the benefit of language. Says Robert, an art teacher: "I love to travel, particularly
when I'm around others who enjoy traveling as well. I also enjoy
sketching and take my sketchpad everywhere. One summer, while I
was on a group tour of Europe, I was sitting across the train from a
woman I found very attractive. I didn't feel comfortable just going
over and striking up a conversation, so I began sketching her. She
smiled at me, and that broke the ice. I found out later that she didn't
speak English, so sketching was the perfect way to break through
the language barrier. In the process, I attracted several other people,
and I was never at a loss for companionship the rest of the trip."

Janet attended a professional seminar in the hopes of meeting some new people. She was unsuccessful in this regard until she volunteered to help set up the room for the seminar. "All of a sudden, I was involved," she says. "I was working with a group of people toward some purpose. There was a natural reason for contact. Later, we all went out together and I still see these people as friends."

By moving from the passive role to taking an active role, Janet increased her own enjoyment of the workshop. She also made herself more visible, and gave people a chance to contact her.

For John, a forty-year-old engineer, playing co-ed soccer has been a way to meet people. "After we've all been out there yelling, screaming, laughing, it's really easy for me to go and talk to anybody I want to." Like Robert, John discovered that when you are absorbed in activity, you don't need to get up your nerve to talk to people, nor do you need flashy moves. Contact just seems to happen spontaneously—and effortlessly. The activity becomes a safe and positive way to let others know you are enjoying their company. As Stanford psychologist Philip Zimbardo says, "The easiest conversations in the world are those where people can talk about their common enthusiasms."

KEY 6

"Want to be even more attractive? Be the kind of person who can turn a less-than-ideal situation into fun."

Laura, a twenty-five-year-old student, reports: "Last spring, I went on a camping trip with an old high school friend and two other people she'd lived with. It rained just about the whole time we were there, but we had a great time anyway. While we were confined to the tent, we read, talked, or played crazy games. When the sun came out, we dried out on the beach, went hiking and mountain climbing. One evening we sat around the fire and sang every song we knew. It was so much fun, we didn't even mind sitting out in the rain. We were having such a raucous good time, that folks from the next two campsites joined in and we made new friends. The next day, it rained again but it didn't matter. We all spent the day playing cards, charades, and just talking."

Janet, the woman who enjoyed assisting at the seminar, says, "When I began creating fun out of nothing it really turned things around for me. I mean, there we were moving chairs and tables, setting up microphones and so on. No fun. So I began laughing and shouting orders at people, being generally outrageous. People caught on, and what had been drudgery became fun. In fact, later on someone came up and personally thanked me for making the work situation such a good time."

You too can probably recall a time when you decided to turn less than ideal circumstances into fun. The people who meet other people most successfully and easily choose to "celebrate" these situations rather than endure them. It isn't always easy to see frustration or disappointment as an opportunity for fun. But when you do, the rewards of going for the good time you deserve far outweigh any negative consequences. Take Jill, for example. She had come to town in September, and had been so absorbed in her school work that she didn't have much time for a social life. Now New Year's Eve was approaching, and she wanted to go dancing. But she didn't have a date. So she called up a couple of woman friends and suggested that they go out to a local dance club; but her friends felt reluctant to go out as "singles" on an evening when everyone else is coupled up. "I'm just going to enjoy a quiet evening at home," one of her friends told her.

But Jill didn't really feel like being at home. She wanted to be out partying and dancing. She did feel odd being a single woman out alone, but she felt more uncomfortable staying home in front of the TV. So she ventured out to a local bar where there were usually a lot of singles. When she walked in, she realized that just about everyone was coupled and her first impulse was to get out of there, retreat to the safety of her home. But she calmed herself and reminded herself of her determination to be out dancing on New Year's Eve. As she moved into the room, she spotted another single woman standing alone at the bar. She made a beeline for the woman, who was a bit put off at first by all this sudden attention. "Look," said Jill, "I'm here alone and I'm a bit anxious. Could I just talk to you for a while?"

The other woman agreed, and it turned out they had a number of friends in common. The other woman was there with a few friends, and she asked Jill to join them. Later on in the evening, Jill was ready to dance. "Come on," she said to her new friend.

"Let's go ask some guys to dance."

"Oh no," the woman said. "I couldn't do that."

"You don't have to do anything," Jill told her. "I'll ask one for you. Just follow me." The other woman reluctantly followed Jill, who by this time had spotted an eligible-looking man. She asked him to dance, he agreed, and it turned out he was there with his brother. Both Jill and her friend enjoyed a number of dances with several different men.

Looking back on the experience, Jill is proud that she persisted in doing what she wanted to do that evening. "It was particularly important to me to have an ally, someone I could feel safe with. When I was talking her into going out on the dance floor, I was really talking to myself. Anyhow, it worked for both of us."

Not only did Jill take the plunge and go for celebrating rather than enduring an evening alone, she put herself squarely in charge of her own good time. Her reward was more than meeting people to dance with. She now has the memory of a really good time that she created for herself without waiting for the perfect person to come along. These experiences work like a growing "bank account" of good feelings that overflow into our lives and our relationships with others. The result is high self-esteem. And this positive opinion we hold of ourselves is transmitted to others.

To reiterate, celebrating life by doing the things you love to do is like giving yourself an "esteem bath." Which activities do you immerse yourself in when you want to take an esteem bath? How do YOU celebrate life? In the next chapter, you'll have an opportunity to choose the things you love to do—and begin to discover your ideal people-meeting situations.

Chapter 3

66What do you love to do?**99**

It's not hard to tell when you're doing what you love to do. Have you ever been so caught up in an activity that you lost track of time, forgot to eat, or failed to notice someone standing and watching you? Have you ever felt so much excitement and laughter coursing through your body, that you felt the next giggle would make you burst? When you are doing what you love to do, your body, mind, and heart are all engaged. You feel wholly involved and flushed with the experience. Ask a few people to tell you about some truly enjoyable experiences, then watch and listen. Their faces light up, their gestures become animated, and you will hear the pleasure and excitement in their voices. They use words like "excited," "playful," "absorbed," "good mood," "screaming and laughing," "relaxed atmosphere," and "stayed up all night without getting tired," and they recall experiences of the past as vividly as if they were happening this minute.

Take some time now and look at your interests and the things YOU love to do. To stimulate your imagination, we've prepared a menu of activities that people we spoke with said they loved to do. Feel free to borrow ideas from this list or add your own.

We suggested in the Introduction that you keep a special notebook to do the exercises in this book and to record other thoughts and ideas that will help you meet people. You can also use it to record your progress. Open your people-meeting notebook now and make the following lists:

STEP ONE: List five activities you currently enjoy doing with other people.

STEP TWO: List five activities you used to and might still enjoy with others.

STEP THREE: List five new activities you think you might enjoy with others in the future.

As you look at the menu of activities and prepare your own list, consider the following questions:

- Do I feel happy and excited every time I think about this activity?
- Do I look forward to doing this activity with positive anticipation?
- Is this something I used to enjoy, but don't really like anymore?
- Is this one of those activities I feel I *ought* to enjoy?
- Do I lose myself in this activity to the extent that I sometimes forget to eat or lose track of time?
- Do others tell me how turned-on I look while I'm involved in this activity?
- Do I feel satisfied and fulfilled after doing it?

MENU OF ENJOYABLE ACTIVITIES

Acrobatics	Archeology
Acting in a play	Art lessons
Aerobic exercise	Astrology
Amusement parks	Automobile clubs, racing
Archery	Backgammon

Backpacking
Barbecues
Belly Dancing
Bicycling
Boating
Bowling
Brewing beer
Bridge-playing
Basketball
Building a house
Cabinetmaking
Camping
Canoeing
Ceramics
Collecting antiques
Computer programming
Conversing with friends
Cooking
Cooking and eating international foods
Costume parties
Country and Western music
Country club parties
Creative writing
Dancing
Debating
Diving
Electronic gadgetry
Exploring new places
Film making
Fishing
Flying
Folkdancing
Furniture refinishing
Fund raising
Gardening

Genealogy
Giving parties
Going on a cruise
Going out to fine restaurants
Going to a baseball game
Going to flea markets, garage sales
Going to a play
Going to comedy clubs
Going to concerts
Going to lectures
Going to religious services
Golfing
Gymnastics
Ham radio operating
Hang gliding
Hanging out at bookstores
Hiking
Horseback riding
Hunting
Ice skating
Jewelry making
Juggling
Kayaking
Kite flying
Knitting
Learning another language
Learning about other cultures
Life drawing
Listening to music
Long talks by candlelight
Lying out on the beach
Magic
Mah-Jongg
Making collages
Metaphysics

Model making
Mountaineering
Pet breeding
Playing games like Scrabble
  and Trivial Pursuit
Photography
Picnics
Playing music
Playing cards
Playing the flute
Playing the piano
Polo
Racquetball
Reading
Riding motorcycles
Rock climbing
Rock collecting
Rodeo
Roller skating
Running
Sailing
Scuba diving
Sculpture
Sewing
Sharing massage
Shelling
Shopping
Sightseeing
Singing
Singing in a choir
Singing rock 'n' roll
Sketching in the park
Skiing
Sky diving
Soaking in a hot tub

Soccer
Social or political activism
Softball
Speaking to groups
Square dancing
Star gazing
Sunbathing
Surfing
Swimming
Taking a class
Taking a clown class
Taking balloon rides
Taking bike trips
Taking long walks
Talking on the CB radio
Target shooting
Teaching a class
Telling jokes
Tennis
Traveling
Visiting art museums
Volleyball
Walking in the woods
Walking your dog
Watching TV with friends
Water skiing
Weaving, spinning
White water rafting
Wind surfing
Wine tasting
Wood carving
Working on cars
Writing stories and poems
Yoga

Next, as part of the adventure of really finding out which activities are for you, go through the activities you have chosen one at a time and, in your mind, live the experience. Begin by picturing yourself involved in the activity. When you have a vivid picture, step inside the picture as if you were trying on new clothes. While you are "in" the activity, notice how you feel. Are you excited? Happy? Enthusiastic? Turned on? Are you bored? Scared? Uncomfortable? Dissatisfied? Feeling good should be your first criterion. If it doesn't feel good, change the experience until it does.

We strongly suggest that you do this exercise now after looking at the list. It should take you about fifteen minutes.

TIPS FOR CHOOSING
YOUR FUN ACTIVITIES

1. Choose only those activities that really excite you. In our seminars, sometimes people say, "I've tried meeting people through common interests, just as you suggest, but it hasn't worked for me." As they elaborate, we find they've almost always failed to distinguish between an "interest" taken up because they think they can meet people that way, and an activity they are truly absorbed in and excited about. When people look for common interests as a way to meet people, they're on the right track. Common interests can serve as a neutral, nonthreatening way to make contact. But if you want that contact with another person to be electric and exciting, do something you absolutely love to do. Are you interested in square dancing, rock climbing, going to concerts? Merely being "interested" is not the same as being totally involved. Find those activities you can pursue with total absorption, passion, and abandon, and you have found the ideal way for you to meet people.

2. Make sure the activity you choose involves others. When you choose an activity you love to do as a way to meet people, obviously you need to go about it in such a way that you can share your experience with others. Take the example that people bring up in seminars all the time: "Suppose what I really love to do is read? How do I meet people then?" Well, you could hang around libraries. But libraries don't really offer an opportunity to communicate with others, because talking is discouraged. A better bet would be to get a job at a bookstore. Or join a reading circle or take a literature class where you can meet others who love to read. The important thing is to share your excitement and enthusiasm with another who is likely to appreciate it—and be attracted to you.

Anything you love can be a means of meeting other people, but it does require a little bit of imagination and the willingness to act. Take George. George loves movies. His favorite movie is *It's a Wonderful Life,* which often plays at a local theater around Christmas time. For the past several years, George has found out when and where the film was playing, and then invited friends and friends of friends to an *It's a Wonderful Life* potluck dinner. After dinner, the entire group troops over to the theater and enjoys the movie. Many people who had never seen the movie before but who now enjoy it have made the event an annual tradition. George gets to share his enthusiasm for the movie with others—and meets people in the process.

Whether you really love tinkering with cars, preparing desserts, studying art, or working with political action groups, your activity can be a way to meet people. Even accounting. Gloria is an accountant and she loves it. She eagerly reads all the latest government regulations so she can figure out ways of saving her clients money. An enjoyable evening for her involves curling up with an accounting textbook. Yet, through accounting, Gloria gets to meet many people. Her clients enjoy being with her because she genuinely enjoys her work. She also speaks to business and social organizations and teaches a community education class on starting your own business. Gloria has no problem meeting people because she loves being an accountant—and has found a way to share her enthusiasm with others.

3. Beware of "oughtism." As you look at the things you truly love to do, do you notice that you give these activities a low priority? Do you find yourself going along with activities you don't really enjoy—like golf and bar-hopping—just because you believe you have to in order to meet people? Do you find yourself doing things because others (or your own sense of propriety) have said you "ought" to do them? "Oughtism"—an all-too-common affliction that causes you to "oughtamatically" put your feelings and desires second—is one of the biggest blocking forces to meeting people comfortably. For just as you are a magnet that attracts people when you are doing what you love to do, you can give confusing messages when you're trying to enjoy things you don't really enjoy. Just the look on your face can give you away.

We take our leisure seriously in this country, perhaps too seriously. Leisure activities are often competitive—to develop better muscles, to show off, to get points on our social report card because we are supposed to do this or that. Keep in mind that when your intention is to meet people and let them see who you really are, trying to have fun or pretending to have fun doesn't work nearly as well as ACTUALLY HAVING FUN. Don't victimize yourself with activities that YOU don't enjoy, and don't let others "oughta" you around either!

In her book, *Go for It*, psychologist Irene Kassorla chides her readers who would put everyone else's desires before their own. Assuming we had five hundred years to live, Kassorla says, we could spend the first hundred pleasing our parents, the next hundred pleasing our kids, the third hundred doing what our friends want us to do, the fourth hundred obeying the wishes of society. The fifth and final hundred years we could finally spend on ourselves. Her point is powerfully made—given the fact that you are not immortal, you must choose how you spend what time you have. And when you spend that time following everyone else's path but your own, resentment is bound to ensue. A psychologist we interviewed said much of the depression he encountered in his patients was caused by people taking care of everyone else first and themselves last. And the antidote to such depression? Finding out what it takes to make yourself feel good—and doing that.

Not that you should never compromise or do things for other people—one of the most joyous parts of being human is giving to others. But it's extremely important that when you are giving, you give out of choice rather than obligation. The people who are most socially successful are those who can freely say yes and freely say no. These people are often able to persist in getting their own needs met.

Follow what you feel. If you feel attracted to an activity, that's a good enough reason to at least investigate it; don't fall into the trap of believing you have to do it perfectly. "I oughta be able to do it perfectly" is just another form of oughtism.

Consider for a moment how we become good at things. For example, there's the little boy who shows an early interest in cars. His father buys him a set of tools and they begin to work on the family car together. By the time the boy is sixteen, he is adept at working on other people's cars as well. Neighbors say he has a "natural knack" for mechanics, but is that really so? He began with an interest and that interest was reinforced. From the time he was small, he was told he was good with cars. That is what he believed about himself. And more and more, it became the case. If you love to do something and don't feel you're great at it, keep doing it. You're bound to get better.

You now know that the easiest and most comfortable way to meet people is to be active, be yourself, have fun and do what you love to do. You have identified some activities you really enjoy and some you might like to try. You have probably also begun thinking about how you can meet more people while skiing, or enjoying concerts, or gardening, or whatever it is you love to do. In the next chapter, you will take the next step toward meeting more of the people you want to meet—identifying just whom you want to meet and why.

Chapter 4

66Knowing who you want to meet and why: developing your social agenda99

You have just found out your best friend is getting married, so you decide to buy a new suit or dress for the wedding. Since this is going to be a gala event, and since this is your very best friend in the world, you naturally want your new clothes to look great and fit perfectly. But there are a lot of demands on your time—your job, your social life, the little things to do around the house. And you really don't enjoy shopping very much either. So you go to the Yellow Pages and look under "Clothing." You call the very first store you find—"Aardvark Department Store" and you ask the person who answers the phone to pick you out a new outfit for the wedding. You're not sure what size you wear, or what color or style you're looking for, so you decide to leave that up to the salesperson. After all, they are the ones who know clothing, so you're absolutely confident they'll come up with just the right thing.

"But don't you want to come in and try it on?" the sales-person asks.

"Oh, that's not necessary," you tell them. "I'm sure it'll work out fine anyway."

Of course this is absurd. You wouldn't dream of buying a new suit or dress without first specifying size, color, and style. You certainly wouldn't buy such an important item without first trying it on to find out how it feels and how it fits, and if it didn't look quite right you would either make adjustments or select another outfit. Yet people often go out to meet people without being clear in their own minds who they want to meet, without communicating what they want, and without "trying on" the experience to see whether it matches what they are looking for. Wouldn't it seem a lot more sat-isfying to look carefully for what you want than to struggle to fit in-to an experience you don't want, are not comfortable in, and might never be happy with?

The people who consistently meet the people THEY want to meet have a clear idea of what they are looking for and what they have to offer. They have a sense of where they're going in life and know what they like and don't like, both in terms of activi-ties and people. Instead of waiting around for the right person or people to come along, socially successful people do two things si-multaneously: they actively pursue the things they love to do, and they use these activities as a bridge to meeting and getting to know new friends. In short, they are pursuing a "social agenda."

Simply defined, having a social agenda means knowing what kinds of people you want to meet and why you want to meet them. But a well-formed social agenda also takes into consideration what you value in life, where you're going, what you love doing, and what you have to offer, as well as specifying the kinds of people you would like to meet. As you'll see later on in the chapter, you may have a number of different social agendas at the same time. Naturally, the more clearly defined your social agenda, the more likely you are to recognize the people you are looking for and the places you are likely to find them.

You have probably noticed the personals columns in newspapers and magazines. Those are social agendas in written form. The best personals ads—those that are the most specific, viv-id, and accurate—inspire responses from the right people (i.e., the people the ad-writer wants to meet). We'll cover how to write per-sonals ads in Chapter Seven, but you don't have to place an ad to put your social agenda out there to potential friends. By formulating what you want and what you have to offer, and choosing the activities where you can have fun and meet people, you will become a walking personals ad—that is, you will be telling people about yourself simply by the activities you choose and the way you pursue those activities. Your activities will also provide an easy way to communicate with new acquaintances and find out whether your social agendas match.

KEY 7

" The better you know yourself, the better your chances for finding people who are right for you. "

One thing is true, regardless of your social agenda: the better you know yourself, the easier it will be to find what you are looking for. All social agendas, therefore, begin with who you are, what you enjoy, and where you are going in life—what we've termed "Life Stage," "Life Course," and "Life-style." Once you know where you are in life (Life Stage), where you are going (Life Course), and how you want to get there (Life-style), it becomes easier to address the questions, "Whom do I want to meet?" and "What role do I want that person to play in my life?" It's also easier to see if your social agenda matches that of a potential partner.

Being aware of differences in these all-important areas will enable you to choose more carefully upfront, select places and situations where you're likely to find a match, and avoid finding out too late that the person you're involved with has charted a Life Course completely different from your own. So before you design your social agendas, let's look at your Life Stage, Life Course, and Life-style.

LIFE STAGE   Jean is divorced and has a thirteen-year-old son. As far as she's concerned, her childbearing years are behind her, yet many of the men she's met are interested in starting their own families. She, on the other hand, is interested in hanging in there until her son finishes high school, and then enjoying the freedom to travel and pursue all the other interests she has postponed. "I recently started going to activities designed for single parents," she says, "and I'm finally meeting men who are in a similar LIFE STAGE."

Where are YOU in life? Is raising a family ahead of you or behind you? Are you ready to put down roots, or do you presently have the travel bug? Are you ready to try something completely different? Or are you cruising until retirement? Your answers to these questions will influence whom you want to bring into your life, what you have to offer, and what roles you'll play in each other's lives.

LIFE COURSE   When he was still a student in college, Charles sat down one day and made a list of all the things he wanted to accomplish in life. The exercise was just for fun, but when he was finished he realized he wanted to see—and live in—as many places as he could in his lifetime. Now, whenever he meets a prospective serious dating partner, he makes it a point to tell her about his projected LIFE COURSE before they get too far into the relationship. "So far, it's worked quite well," he says. "I usually end up with someone interested in the same kinds of things, or someone who understands we're dating on a casual basis. I also find that the places I choose to go to meet people—around activities I love—tend to attract women more interested in adventure."

Where do you see yourself going in life? Do you plan to spend two years in the Peace Corps? Eight years in medical school? Twenty years in the Air Force? Do you see yourself living a quiet life in the country, or in a high rise in New York City? Is there a trip around the world in your future? Or would you be just as happy driving half a mile to the PTA meeting once a month? Even though life is full of surprises and there's no way to know exactly what you'll be up to five years from now, chances are you have a sense of where you are headed. If you're expecting to find long-term traveling companions, be sure your social agenda reflects your LIFE COURSE.

LIFE-STYLE   About four years ago, Pam left her small hometown in the Southwest to take a job in a large East-Coast city. "The first year," she recalls, "I was miserable. Everything was so fast-paced, so urban. The men I met were all trying to impress me with things I'm just not impressed by. But in a way it was good, because it forced me to look at the kind of life-style I wanted to lead. I realized that I love the wide open spaces, so I joined a hiking and backpacking club. I've also gone on a number of ski weekends, and I've noticed I'm much more myself—and more likely to meet my kind of people—at these outdoorsy kinds of things. I also started attending church again, and I find these more low-key activities a really welcome change from the hustle and bustle."

How do you want to live your life? Are you blue jeans and flannel shirt—or Gucci loafers and Perrier? Do you dream of a huge lawn to mow in the suburbs, or would you prefer restoring a brownstone in the city? Are you an incurable jock? Or would you rather be playing Scrabble? Do you enjoy large parties, or intimate gatherings with a few friends? The more you meet people through the activities you love, the more likely you are to find matching LIFE-STYLES.

Take a few moments now to summarize in your notebook your Life Stage, Life Course, and Life-style. These may change over time, but don't worry about that. The important thing is to know "where you are coming from" and "where you are going to" as of right now. Ask yourself: What's most important to me right now about my Life Stage, Life Course, Life-style? What implications does that have for the people I want to meet and what I have to offer them? Some sample Life Stage statements include: "I am recently divorced and not ready for a serious relationship right now." "I have never been married and want to find someone to start a family with." "My main priority now is making it in my career, and any relationship I'm in will have to support that goal."

Some sample Life Course statements include: "When I finish grad school in three years, I will be moving to Colorado." "My main goal in life is to be a professional dancer. Dance is my first loyalty and my ultimate 'marriage partner.' " "I don't see myself moving around a lot—once I meet the right person, I plan to stay in one place and build my life there."

Life-style statements include: "Whatever I end up doing in life, wherever I live, I MUST be around artists or other creative people." "Money—and the things money buys—are very important to me. I'm all for the two-career, two-income family." "My religious faith is very important to me, so of course anyone I end up with must be able to support and enhance this faith."

Your Life Stage, Life Course, Life-style statements have provided you with a framework for knowing yourself. To flesh out the skeleton, let's look at two other factors—what you have to offer to other people, and what you love to do. Susan, a twenty-five-year-old nurse, reports: "I was feeling depressed about meeting people a while back. My attitude was, 'What's the use?' A friend suggested that I try writing a personals ad, so I began to look at these ads more carefully. I noticed that the ads I found most appealing always men-

tioned what the person who placed the ad could bring to a relationship. So I made a list of my own best traits, and I felt better immediately. I realized I had a lot to offer. Even though I chickened out on
placing the ad, my whole perspective changed. I said to myself,
'Hey, I'm a catch!' "

     As Susan found out, immersing yourself in what you have
to offer is like taking an "esteem bath." Not only does it increase
your confidence in your ability to attract and sustain relationships,
but it can give you a clue as to the kinds of people who might be
looking for what you have to offer. Susan, for example, realized
that one thing she valued in herself was her unwavering loyalty to
friends and lovers. Unfortunately, her primary way of meeting men
had been in bars, where a trait like loyalty would be likely overlooked in favor of physical attributes. "I decided to do two things,"
she says. "First, I would remind myself of my positive qualities before going out anywhere I was likely to meet people. I also decided
to spend more of my time in settings where people could get to
know me over time."

     What special traits and attributes do you bring to a
friendship or love relationship? Make a list of those in your notebook now, and feel free to add to or modify the list. An excellent
way to "prime the pump" is to ask close friends, family, or trusted
co-workers what they think your most positive traits are. To further
stimulate your thinking, we've included a partial list:

MENU OF POSITIVE TRAITS

Accepting of others	Healthy
Adventurous nature	Honest
Affectionate	Independent
Care about others	Know how to have a good time
Communicate easily	Know how to draw out others
Creative	Love to learn
Easy to talk to	Loyal
Enthusiastic	Open minded
Friendly	Perceptive
Good listener	Positive attitude
Great at problem solving	Reliable

Respectful of others	Sense of humor
Responsive	Thoughtful
Self-reliant	Well-groomed

Now you've made a list of your positive traits, but suppose instead of feeling positive and optimistic, you feel more frustrated than when you began? "It's great that I have all of these stunning attributes," you say, "but where I go to meet people, no one ever gets to find out about them!" Which brings us back to the things you love to do. You need an arena to let people know who you are and what you have to offer. And the best way to be yourself and broadcast who you are (and find others on the same wavelength) is through your favorite activities. Go back to your list of fun activities from Chapter Three and find those that excite you most. Include those in your list of those assets you have to offer.

You now know where you are in your life, where you're going, and how you'd like to get there. You have an idea of the special qualities you can bring to a friendship or relationship, including the things you love to do. You are now ready to explore the other half of your social agenda: those people you want to meet and why.

KEY 8

"Knowing what you're looking for makes it easier to find the people you want to meet in the natural flow of life."

There is an old Chinese saying, "When you do not know where you are going, you are likely to end up there." Fortunately, the reverse is true as well—when you do know where you're going, it's a lot easier to get to the right place.

The first step in knowing where you'd like to go is identifying the areas of your life you'd like to "people." While each individual must decide which social agendas to pursue, all social agendas reflect one or all of the following needs: to belong to a community, to be affiliated with a social group, to have close friends and extended family, and to share life with an intimate partner.

COMMUNITY The mailperson, the people at the Laundromat, your children's teacher, your minister or rabbi, your neighbors, the people you smile at or say hello to each day, all combine to give you a sense of community. Without the comfort, connection, and sense of belonging community provides, people feel alienated or discouraged, as if no one cares. A sense of being in a community is a foundation for other groups we belong to and other people we get to meet. Social needs around community might include: "I want to meet more of my neighbors so that I find common interests which could be the basis of friendship." "I want to create a positive feeling in our neighborhood so that the streets will stay cleaner"; or "I want to be friendly with more people all day, so that by the time I get to work I'm feeling good." Community is important because the people who are nodding acquaintances, or even strangers, today may become tomorrow's friends. By simply smiling and being friendly, thoughtful, and helpful, by saying hello to the people you see every day and letting them say hello back, you are laying the groundwork for making new acquaintances and maybe even new friends.

ACQUAINTANCES Acquaintances are the people you share activities, interests, and affiliation with. The people you work with, the people on your softball team, the bridge club, the friends you invite to parties, the people you see see every month at the union local, the other parents at the toddler center, the neighbors who invite you to their barbecue, all these constitute your circle of acquaintances. Contact with these people tends to center around specific activities. Chances are you know most of them by name and have a number of things in common.

Acquaintances further reinforce your sense of belonging and being a part of a social fabric. These are the folks you share enjoyable activities with, and the pool of people you most often choose your closest friends from. Therefore, no matter what your social agendas are, it's extremely important that you expand your circle of acquaintances. Some social agendas focusing on acquaintances include: "I would like to find other mothers of preschool children so that we can share ideas and form a play group," "I would like to find a group of people to take bike trips with," or "I would like to join a trade association so I can make business contacts."

CLOSE FRIENDS AND EXTENDED FAMILY
These are the people you share your personal life with, and who share theirs with you. Unlike acquaintances, whom you know pri-

marily through activities and interests, your close friends and extended family are there for you on an ongoing basis. These are the people you are in close contact with almost daily, the people with whom you share your feelings, experiences, ambitions, needs, and desires. A recent study at the University of California at Berkeley has linked the richness of our close social ties with our emotional, and even physical, well-being. Some agendas dealing with close friends and extended families are: "I want to find a friend I can take long trips with, who shares my enthusiasm for nature," "I would like to reconvene the family reunions we used to have when I was a child, so I can be around people who have known me all my life," or "I would like to find another single man or woman I can share triumphs and frustrations with as I search for a mate." Usually close friends emerge out of the people already in our circle of acquaintances, so if you're looking for more friends, you'll want to increase the number of people you meet through activities.

SPOUSE, MATE, OR SPECIAL FRIEND   This is the person you share your most intimate feelings with. Although you may be intimate with close friends, your spouse, mate, or special friend is your partner in life and someone you may choose to start a family with. This kind of relationship can be the most fulfilling and satisfying of all human experiences. Social agendas focusing on a spouse or mate can include: "I would like to find someone who is caring and enjoys children so we can have a family," "I would like to find a woman who loves the outdoors so we can homestead in Montana," or "I would like to find a life partner who is also a professional, so we can live well, make lots of money, and have kids later only if we feel like it."

Chances are, many of you bought this book because you are looking for an intimate relationship. Yet people commonly ask for too much from that one person they choose to share their lives with. How often have you heard people say (or have said yourself), "I wish I had a boyfriend/girlfriend to share such-and-such with"? Of course, it is wonderful and enormously satisfying to share your personal life with another person, but it can be very frustrating to postpone your life until you have found Ms. or Mr. Right. In fact, we have found time and time again that people most often meet their intimate partners in the course of pursuing enjoyable activities and even other social agendas. So don't narrow yourself to just one social agenda. The more contacts you have in each of these social "worlds," the greater your chances will be of meeting someone who will match.

One of the problems many people experience in finding "the right person"—and one of the reasons people settle for relationships that are less than satisfying—is that they tend to do their choosing from far too small a group. That's why we suggest pursuing all aspects of these social agendas simultaneously. Not only will you enjoy a wide range of activities, but you will be meeting more people and therefore dramatically increasing your chances of meeting the people YOU want to meet.

WHO DO YOU WANT TO MEET?

Once you know the areas in your life you want to bring more people to, the next step is to take a careful look at the kinds of people you want to meet. Some people feel uncomfortable being specific about whom they want to meet. "Meeting people is not like ordering items on a pizza," one person told us. "I don't want to do anything that will ruin the spontaneity of meeting someone new." We couldn't agree more. People are much more than lists of ingredients, and if life went exactly as planned, there wouldn't be any fun in living it. However, having a plan can often enhance the chemistry, fun, magic, and drama of meeting others. You've heard the saying, "Luck is the crossroads where preparation and opportunity meet." If you want to be luckier when it comes to meeting people, be prepared—have a clear idea of what and whom you're looking for. A clear social agenda can mean the difference between just enjoying yourself and enjoying yourself while meeting the people you want to meet. Don't worry about spontaneity. Musicians admit that the more they've practiced the easier it is for them to improvise. Have a well-formed social agenda and you will find yourself spontaneously bringing more of the people you want to meet into your life.

Try the following steps for formulating your social agenda: First, to help you decide what kinds of people you really enjoy, list five people you like or have liked in the past and what it is you like or have liked about each person. You might list several things or just one thing about each person. The key here is to be brief and write whatever comes to mind. Take a few minutes to think about each person, and remember back to the good times. If you can, remember a particular time you enjoyed. After you've made your list, summarize all the positive traits you found in the people you liked in a statement that starts with "I have liked people who----" until you have a statement that you can say comfortably (e.g., "I like people who are thoughtful, healthy, like jazz, like cats, etc.").

Next, list five people you do not like or people you have not liked in the past, and what you didn't like about each person. Now add up all these statements into one statement of negative traits: "I don't like people who----" (e.g., "I do not like people who are cruel, wear preppie clothes, gossip, etc."). Again, you will have completed this when you can say the statement comfortably.

Next list five people you are neutral about, and which characteristics they have that don't affect you one way or the other. Again, add all these statements into one statement of neutral traits that reads "I feel neutral about people who----" (e.g., "I feel neutral about people who drive sports cars, like dogs, have beards, are in business for themselves, etc."). It may seem strange to list people and traits you feel neutral about, but this is a very important step.

The positive, negative, and neutral steps are all necessary for you to determine exactly what your "boundaries" are. One of the chief obstacles people encounter in going out to meet new people is their fear that they will not be able to control their situation, that they will be railroaded by other people pushing their own social agendas. This is particularly true of women, whose traditional social role has been to go along with what a man has planned.

Here's where identifying the neutral traits and situations as well as the negative ones comes in handy. Often, when we want to be "nice" or don't want to make a fuss, we try to convince ourselves that we feel neutral about something we really dislike. For example, you're being interviewed for a job and the interviewer smokes. You absolutely detest cigarette smoke and you want to throw up on the carpet. But you also detest being unemployed, so you smile a sickly, polite smile and tell yourself you are neutral about it.

Fortunately, most social situations are not as obviously awkward as that one. Nevertheless, it can be quite uncomfortable to express—even to yourself—negative feelings about a situation. That is why it is so important to distinguish between negative and neutral traits and situations. Writing these down will allow you to see the difference between what you don't like and what you don't care about either way. A neutral column filled with genuinely neutral traits will serve as an alarm that will sound as soon as you try to shift a negative item into neutral.

The neutral list will seve another purpose as well—it will help you distinguish between what is merely "okay" or "tolerable" and what really turns you on. We sometimes settle for less than what we want in a situation or relationship because we don't think we can have what we REALLY want. As you compare your "neutral" list and your "positive" list, notice the differences. And be aware of those times when you DID meet people who embodied those most positive traits. If it happened before, chances are good it will happen again!

You probably already have a good idea of your boundaries—the people and situations you automatically rule out (e.g., murderers, thieves, child beaters, drug dealers, con artists, any person or situation that will put your life and health in jeopardy). We cannot overemphasize how important it is to clearly state what you DO NOT WANT as well as what you do want. Setting and communicating your personal boundaries—and gracefully getting out if they are violated—will enable you to meet and enjoy those people and situations you do like because you will no longer be afraid to say no to those that you do not like.

Now that you have distinguished between which traits you like and dislike and set some boundaries, let's look at what the primary focus of your relationships might be. Are you wanting to find a new mate, companion, or potential spouse? Are you looking for some new friends to share your recreational and social life with? Are you interested in joining new social activity circles to get back into action as a single person? Do you want to meet people because you've just moved to a new community and want to feel at home? You may have lots of reasons for wanting to meet people; spell these out in a list until you can say them comfortably out loud.

A very important step here is to ask yourself what having a certain sort of relationship or knowing a certain sort of person will do for you. Sometimes, we fall into the trap of going after something we don't want, don't need, or that is just not appropriate for our situation, because we used to want it, because other people want it, or because we think we ought to want it.

Jay, who got married at twenty-two upon graduating college and then divorced four years later, told us, "Why did I get married? Because that's what you did. There was nothing to think about. That's what it seemed like people did to begin their lives as adults, so I did it, too. It was right there in the 'manual.' " So before you say you want to meet a certain kind of person for a particular relationship, ask yourself what you are likely to get out of it. If this seems selfish, consider that the best relationships are ones where there is mutual gain. Certainly, the other person should benefit from the relationship, but don't neglect yourself either. A one-sided relationship will ultimately be unsatisfying.

Once you have looked at WHY you want what you want and are satisfied that you really want it, you can make the full statement: "I want to meet people who -------- and are not -------- so that we can --------."

For example:

"I would like to meet someone who is intellectual, mature, and a nature lover and is not cranky, overweight, and a workaholic so that we can get married and have a family."

"I would like to find other musicians who are talented, good communicators, enjoy bluegrass music, and are not on drugs, on ego trips, or playing in another band regularly, so that we can form a band that plays locally two to four nights a week."

"I am looking for someone to practice speaking French with, who is from France, patient, stimulating, and not a chauvinist or judgmental, so that I can improve my French and maybe make a new friend."

"I am looking for a lover who is free-spirited, open, flexible, has a sense of humor, and is not looking for a marriage partner right now, is not financially dependent or negative about men, so we can have a good time and get to know each other in a nonpressured way."

YOUR FULLY DEVELOPED SOCIAL AGENDA

Earlier in the chapter we mentioned personals ads as an excellent way to bring to focus where you are in life, what you're looking for, whom you would like to meet, and what you have to offer. Take the time now to write a personals ad as a way of capturing your social agenda. You may have several different unrelated agendas—for example, to find a dating partner or mate, make business contacts, find racquetball or bridge partners. Write the sample ad for your most important agenda first, then write ads for your other social agendas.

Even if you never place the ad, by being aware of your social agenda as you go out and do the things you love to do, you will automatically be "living" the ad and communicating it. Remember, you don't have to publish the ad for it to work, so be free and frank in stating what you want.

TIPS FOR DEVELOPING YOUR AD

1. Check the personals in your local newspaper, magazine, or singles' publication. Which of these ads describe people who might be interesting to you? Are there other ads that describe people who don't seem like your type, but are good ads anyway? What do the more appealing ads seem to have in common? Which ads seem vague, dull, or downright tacky? What is unappealing about those ads?

2. Look at enough ads to know what you like and what you don't like. Then begin to pull together the information to write your own ad. Make sure your ad reflects:

- Your Life Stage, Life Course, Life-style, and how these relate to what and whom you are looking for
- Your most appealing traits
- Your love-to-dos
- The traits you desire in others, those you are neutral about, and the ones you want to avoid
- The roles you would like your new acquaintances to play in your life, i.e., the kinds of relationships you are looking for and what mutual gains are likely from these relationships.

3. In writing your own ad, go back over the ads you liked. Look for words, phrases, ideas that you find interesting or inspiring. Can any of these be applied to you? Do they stimulate you to describe yourself? If you're stuck on which words to use to describe yourself, ask your friends for words that capture YOU.

4. Be as specific as possible. Specify both who you are and what you want. If you're looking for a life partner, don't say you are looking for someone to play tennis with. If you are looking for casual dates, don't give the impression that you seek a marriage partner. Use words that are "alive"—that is, words that evoke feelings or relate to the senses. Chances are if a word evokes feelings in you it will in someone else, particularly someone to whom you're likely to relate well.

5. Review and modify your ad periodically. One way to get feedback on the ad is to publish it. As one of the women we spoke with told us, "In my first ad, I used the phrase 'to share good times and bad.' I realized that it might have been a mistake to say 'and bad' because I attracted all these guys who wanted to tell me their troubles." But you need not publish your ad to get feedback. "I thought I wanted to meet someone who came from a similar background—you know, shared past experiences and all that," Charles said. "So I began going with someone who had had very similar life experiences. The only trouble was, she was still back there while I had changed."

6. **Look at your personals ad/social agenda several times a week.** It will remind you of what you are looking for, and may offer ideas as to where to find it. By all means communicate your ad/social agenda to others, but only communicate what you feel comfortable telling them. Beware of reading new acquaintances a "laundry list." We will have more to say about communicating your social agenda in Chapter Six. Whether or not you choose to use the personals ad format, we strongly recommend that you write out a social agenda statement to be updated regularly. This statement can later be boiled down to a personals ad, either for publication or for brevity's sake. Here are some examples of fully developed social agendas.

WOMAN, AGE FORTY-TWO, SOCIAL WORKER

1. **LIFE STAGE.** I'm a forty-two-year-old woman, just out of a relationship, looking for one that will lead to marriage. Because of age, opportunity for biological family is over, but would consider adoption. (Being a stepmother feels intimidating.)

2. **LIFE COURSE.** Since I've already "proven" myself in my career, I'd like to phase out of full-time work, be more of a homemaker and do more volunteer work. I don't want the full emotional and financial support of myself.

3. **LIFE-STYLE.** I'm basically a homebody. I like a warm home atmosphere, a two-story white house by a lake. My life-style is simple but clean and orderly, although I'm not compulsive. I also need involvement outside the home, in the theater for example. I like going out, particularly when there's a home to come back to.

4. APPEALING TRAITS. I'm outgoing and friendly, initiate interactions easily. If I'm your friend, I'll always be your friend. I'm happy, secure, independent. I'll spend hours in a card shop looking for just the right card for someone I care about. I'm happy when others are happy.

5. LOVE-TO-DOS. Love to go to theater, watch sports, play the piano. I love gardening and caring for indoor plants, movies (Mary Poppins, Disney fantasies), racquetball. I also love to be treated well.

6. TRAITS I WANT. I want someone who respects me for having a mind, who respects my morals and values, who is reliable (e.g., calls when he says he will), honest, secure, knows where he is going in life, has direction/plans/goals, is willing to share household responsibilities.

7. TRAITS I DON'T WANT. I don't want someone who takes me for granted or is threatened by me, someone who "plays games," is sloppy, overly absorbed in work, inflexible, a noncommunicator; someone who has unresolved feelings about a previous relationship, or can't break away from family of origin, or is utterly materialistic.

8. MY GOAL. I want a happy marriage, primarily one of mutual respect and trust, where we can be ourselves and grow independently as well as together; to be with someone who possesses complementary traits, and interests that I may not yet have but might benefit from. I want to be able to cut back on work and devote myself to the house and more enjoyable occupations.

MAN, AGE THIRTY-TWO, ATTORNEY

1. LIFE STAGE. I'm single and thirty-two. I've just made a decision to concentrate my efforts on doing things rather than just thinking about them. I've decided to open a bar and a franchise company, and this gives me more energy. When I talk about my projects, I'm more excited myself, and more of "me" comes through. I see my life as an adventure, so the special person I want to meet must be both supportive and independent, a partner more than a housewife. I also want friends to enjoy my adventures with.

2. LIFE COURSE. I plan on staying in this town, settling down and getting married, and concentrating on getting myself established.

3. LIFE-STYLE. I want to travel through Austria on a motorcycle in the springtime with a special person, have enough money to do what I want, when I want; have a vacation place up north, go to Aspen, have a boat on the lake.

4. APPEALING TRAITS. I believe I have sensitivity, generosity, gentleness, good sense of humor, am loving and caring.

5. LOVE-TO-DOS. Music, hunting, dancing, camping, fishing—anything outdoors.

6. TRAITS I WANT. Self-confidence and ability to relate to all kinds of people; tolerance and accepting attitude, warmth, and friendliness. The main thing is that they don't judge other people.

7. TRAITS I DON'T WANT. Prejudices, wanting others to think they are "big shooters"; not letting me get a word in edgewise. I lack tolerance for people who lack tolerance.

8. MY GOALS. I am happy with my life—rich or broke, it doesn't matter. I would like to find friends to have a good time with, who will stay loyal no matter what my circumstances, who are "doers" with open minds. I am also looking for a marriage partner who is independent enough to bring something to the relationship other than support for me. I want to be with a woman who enjoys the good life and is willing to work with me to achieve it.

WOMAN, AGE THIRTY, DESIGNER

1. LIFE STAGE. I'm in a transition right now, having just started my own business. I'm deciding on where I want to live and work, based on work opportunities, where potential mates are, and where my friends are. I'm looking for a life partner with mutual professional interests, someone who is "mainstream" yet is spiritually oriented. I need a person with a sense of tradition and who wants to have a family.

2. LIFE COURSE.   I'm looking at moving to another area, going back to school, continuing my design practice, finding a mate, and getting myself stronger physically, spiritually, emotionally, intellectually.

3. LIFE-STYLE.   I want to live in a city, on the water, and the city should have both a sense of energy and a sense of calmness, with many social and career options. I would love a gorgeous apartment with a view.

4. APPEALING TRAITS.   I have enthusiasm, tenderness, compassion, and creative vision.

5. LOVE-TO-DOS.   I like to feel that my mind, body, and spirit are working together. I like talking with friends, dancing, touching, hugging, and making love, back rubs, creating designs, making things beautiful.

6. TRAITS I WANT.   I want someone who is patient, compassionate, open, honest, and intelligent.

7. TRAITS I DON'T WANT.   Stinginess; someone who is manipulative, tight, inarticulate, or boring; someone who is locked in and doesn't care about moving forward; people who won't share their feelings; playboys and extreme "new-agey" types.

8. MY GOALS.   A trusting and secure environment so that I have the opportunity to blossom and an opportunity to support another person, as well. I want to create a situation—in my work life and with another person—where growth is infectious, and support for one another snowballs.

As you can see, social agendas—and how they are expressed—may differ greatly from one person to the next. Yours may look nothing like any of the ones we have presented. Just make sure you write something under each of the topic areas, even if you're not totally sure of what you are looking for or what you have to offer. You will become clearer about your social agenda the more you meet and interact with new people. It's a good idea to refer to your social agenda regularly to see how well your social experiences match what you want, and modify them accordingly.

We recommend that you make a "movie" in your mind of how your social agenda might look when achieved. Make the movie full of vivid colors and beautiful sounds so you can enjoy it fully even before you achieve it. Use this mental picture as a way of making sure what you are asking for is really what you want. Look at your social agenda statement as a compass that lets you know whether or not you are "on course." Your social agenda will be the main way for you to qualify the people and situations you want in your life, and carefully select only those you really want. Your social agenda may be the most valuable thing you can get out of this book because the key to a full and satisfying social life is choice. And a fully developed social agenda is the first step toward choosing wisely.

Chapter 5

"Why you need a social agenda"

       You may think that creating a social agenda sounds like a lot of work, but much of the frustration we experience in trying to meet suitable people can be traced to NOT formulating and pursuing a clear social agenda. To illustrate the unfortunate consequences of not having a well-developed social agenda, we present here a number of "horror stories" we heard in the course of our interviews. As you grit your teeth and read, you may identify with some of the unfortunates in the stories. Don't stop reading. Antidotes will follow!

HORROR STORY 1

MAN LURED INTO SINGLES' COMPLEX—NEARLY DIES OF FRUSTRATION!

John, a recently divorced man in his late thirties, was moving to a new town to begin a new job. When he told the real estate agent he was looking for a place where there were plenty of activities and single people, the agent said he had just the thing. "There's this new complex that just opened up," he said, "and it has tennis courts, a pool, and a rec room where people have parties at least four nights a week. And just about everyone there is single." This sounded perfect to John. He visited the place briefly during the day, and it appeared to be everything the agent had promised. He moved in.

Over the first few weeks, John went to a number of parties, swam at the pool, and played tennis with some of the residents, only to find that most of the people were much younger than he was and that he didn't have much in common with them. John has been a world traveler and feels at home in different cultures. Most of the people he was meeting at the singles' complex were recent graduates just starting out at their jobs. They were mainly in their early twenties and spent a lot more time partying than John wanted to. While he had no trouble making contact with people, he found his encounters at the complex "empty and just not satisfying." He began to wonder if he would ever find people who were right for him.

ANTIDOTE FOR HORROR STORY 1: A SOCIAL AGENDA SPELLS OUT WHAT PEOPLE YOU WANT TO MEET.

Just as you would specify the size, color, and style of a suit or dress you were buying, so it is important to specify the kinds of people you would like to meet. In telling the real estate agent that he wanted to meet single people, John failed to specify such essential elements as life stage, life course, life-style.

Many of the other people we spoke with who recounted stories of unsuccessful encounters also had vague social agendas. The women who tell their friends, "I'd like to meet men" are taking the first small step. But unless they add some qualifications to that statement (e.g., "I'd like to meet eligible men who like children") they are likely to feel frustrated as they are introduced to one man after another who just isn't right for them.

KEY 9

"When you know what you want, you'll know when you've found it."

When you take the simple step of stopping to think about and write down what you are looking for as specifically as you can you take the first step toward your goal. Having a social agenda adds a dimension of awareness to your everyday life. A case in point is Lynette, who sat down and wrote a detailed description of the man she wanted to meet. She included physical appearance, attitudes, life-style, common interests. "I had read about that exercise in a book," she says, "and I even knew someone who'd used it successfully. But I just did it to find out what I was looking for. I was extremely skeptical about it working." Less than two weeks later, she was introduced to a man at an outdoor concert. In the course of a brief conversation, she found that he had a lot of the attributes she was looking for. As he was leaving, she impulsively went up to him and asked to continue the conversation. They ended up talking continuously for the next four hours, taking a trip together later that summer, and getting married. "The reason I was able to take that risk," Lynette says, "was that he fit what I was looking for so completely. If it weren't for making that list, though, I might have let him get away."

Says Greta, a thirty-one-year-old writer, "When I went to college, I found myself at a large school not knowing anyone. But I did know the kind of person I wanted to have as a friend—someone who was interesting and came from a background similar to mine. The first day, I met a woman who lived across the hall in the dorm who also came from a large Catholic family and grew up out in the country. I hastily arranged to have her switch with someone else and move into my dorm room. Thirteen years later, she is still my best friend."

When you know what you want, you are more likely to put yourself in a situation where you might find it, and you are more likely to communicate your agenda to others. Having a clearly formed social agenda is an important step, but it is equally important to go where people who match that social agenda are most likely to be. Which brings us to Horror Story #2:

HORROR STORY 2

WOMAN GOES TO BAR TO FIND MALE FRIEND; LEAVES ALONE AND DISGUSTED.

Alice has recently ended a long-term relationship. Although she is not yet ready for a romantic involvement with a man, she is looking for some male friends who might eventually turn into romantic prospects. In fact, she has a very clear idea of the kind of man she would like to meet—sensitive, intelligent, playful, and above all, someone who will respect her desire for friendship first. Problem is, Alice has not been able to find this man. Each Friday evening, she goes to the local bar with her friends, where she waits and waits until some man comes over to talk with her. When he does, he usually is after sex and not at all interested in her desire for friendship. Sometimes she sees someone she might like to talk to, but she can't seem to make herself move and make contact. Needless to say, she has concluded that there just aren't any men around who are interested in her as a person, and if there are, she doesn't know how to find them.

ANTIDOTE FOR HORROR STORY 2: MATCH THE SITUATION WITH YOUR SOCIAL AGENDA.

Don't expect to hear Mozart in a honky tonk bar. Alice is looking in exactly the wrong place for the kind of man she wants. There is always the possibility she will find him at a singles' bar, but it's not probable. She would do better to choose an activity she enjoys where she can pursue her social agenda over time. She has falsely concluded that there are no appropriate men, when in fact she just hasn't discovered where to look for them. If you're meeting the "wrong" people, perhaps you're looking in the wrong places.

KEY 10

"The easiest way to meet people is to combine your social agenda with your favorite activities."

As we keep repeating until we're blue in the face, the place to find people you like is doing the things you like to do. Here are some examples of how this works:

When Rick and Sally moved to New York, they found themselves in a big city where they didn't know anyone. Says Rick, "Since I love to entertain, I decided to throw a housewarming party and invite all the people my friends told me to look up in New York. Although some people we did know came from out of town, most of the guests at the party were strangers. We also used the party as an opportunity to go around the building and invite our neighbors. I understand that this just isn't done in New York, but we did it anyway and it worked. Most of the neighbors were friendly, and a number of them came to the party. Everyone had a great time and we ended up making some new friends."

What Sally and Rick did was combine their enjoyment of entertaining with their social agenda—to meet new friends in a new city. The plan worked because they were doing something they loved to do—throwing a party. The guests saw Rick and Sally at their best, and later invited them to their parties. But without a social agenda, the event wouldn't have been nearly as successful. Rick and Sally might have decided to have a dinner party for just the small group of people they already knew. Instead, they combined their good time with a goal—and were doubly successful.

Margaret enjoys playing tennis. Almost by accident, she discovered how she could combine tennis with another of her social agendas—meeting men to go out with. Says Margaret, "When I meet a man I might be interested in, I ask him if he plays tennis. If he says yes, it's the easiest thing in the world to suggest getting together for a match. I've gotten to play a lot more tennis, and I've gotten to know a number of men in a safe, relaxed way. I never realized that asking men out could be so easy."

Steve makes a habit of spending part of each Saturday morning at the local farmer's market. "Even though it only takes a few minutes to do the shopping," he says, "I make it a point to stroll around the area for an hour or so looking for people I know. During my leisurely Saturday shopping, I've made dates, confirmed business deals, found out where the parties were that night, and gotten to know people I'd already met. I'd been talking to this one woman at the market for months. Finally, the last time I saw her there I asked her out."

What these people all learned—either by happy accident or by conscious design—is that nothing could be easier than pursuing your social agenda while doing what you really enjoy. You are alert to the possibilities of finding the kind of person you are looking for, yet you are also absorbed in other activities. These enjoyable activities provide you with a relaxed arena to get to know people at your own pace. In this sense, a social agenda can mean more than meeting new people—it can mean getting to know better those people you've already met.

Dave, a computer programmer, speaks of the "multiple context." "I met this woman at a training and development seminar where she was handing out her résumés. I realized I had seen her before at a computer conference. This, of course, made it easier for me to go up and say, 'Didn't I meet you before at the software convention?' " This also builds trust and rapport. Not only do you become more familiar with people the second time you meet them, but you begin to see areas you have in common.

Another simple yet very effective way of pursuing your social agenda is by being friendly. It takes no effort to smile, nod, to say hello to people you see on the street, particularly those people you see regularly. Says Gloria, a thirty-four-year-old accountant, "I recently realized that an excellent way to attract new friends is by being friendly. At one time, I pooh-poohed this because I felt it would make me seem too eager. But then I realized that the kind of person I would like to meet is just the kind of person who would be attracted by friendliness."

As we said earlier, it is just as important to know what you DON'T want as what you DO want. But simply knowing isn't enough. You must clearly communicate your social agenda, or else someone else's social agenda will take precedence. Traditionally, women have been trained to let men make the decisions, and many men—and women—still abide by this custom. Fortunately, more and more women are willing to communicate what they want. Had Joyce stated her preferences, she might have avoided . . .

HORROR STORY 3

WOMAN TRAPPED WITH BORING DATE FOR SIX HOURS; "I WAS AFRAID IT WOULD NEVER END," SHE SAYS.

Joyce, thirty-two, was called up and invited to dinner by a man she had met briefly the week before. He seemed like a "pretty nice guy," so she accepted. An hour before he was supposed to pick her up, the man called to say he wasn't hungry and wanted to go downtown to his favorite club to listen to jazz. Even though Joyce is not particularly fond of jazz, she figured she probably could endure it. (Remember that word from the last chapter?) She endured it, but barely. "He was boring, the jazz was boring, the place was boring, and the whole evening was a waste," she says. "I know that when I accept a date with someone I don't really know, the worst that can happen is that I have a bad time. In this case, the worst happened."

ANTIDOTE FOR HORROR STORY 3: BE SPECIFIC ABOUT WHAT YOU ENJOY DOING, AND COMMUNICATE THIS.

Joyce made a major error that resulted in a not very fun evening. As many people do, Joyce discounted what SHE wanted to do. Not wanting to seem overly aggressive or demanding, she let someone else's social agenda take precedence over her own. Listening to jazz is not one of her favorite activities. Yet she didn't specifically let her date know how she felt beforehand, nor did she suggest an alternative. She could have said, "You know, I'm not very excited about listening to jazz, but there's this movie I've been dying to see . . ." One of the main reasons people endure unsatisfying activities—and relationships—is because they feel they don't have any choice. Deciding what YOU want to do and communicating it gives you that choice.

KEY 11

"The more clearly you communicate what you want, the more likely you are to find it!"

When it comes to going out and meeting people, one of the biggest problems—particularly for women—is setting boundaries. Says Carol, thirty-seven, "I had literally stopped going out for several months because the men I was meeting all seemed wrong for me. I'd meet a guy, he'd ask me out, and just about immediately he'd expect sexual intimacy. For me, it takes a lot more time and getting to know someone. My reaction was to shut down, and the guys would get angry as if I had led them on. This happened at least three times. So I didn't go out for a while. On the advice of a friend, I began telling men I met as soon as it was appropriate that I wasn't interested in casual sex and it takes me a while to get close. I was surprised at the results. A few of the men I never heard from again. The two that I have gone out with have been very nice to me and respectful of the boundaries I set up. One told me he appreciated my saying where I was right up front. I feel much more in charge and much more willing to get close—at my own pace."

As Carol discovered, there is a way to communicate your social agenda and boundaries in a firm yet friendly way. This communication, difficult as it may be at first, becomes more graceful, less awkward, with practice. There's no need to sacrifice the joys of human contact by going along with something you don't really want. You and any dating partner should agree right away that you both will express your preferences regarding activities. Whenever anyone balks at this, consider it a "red flag" meaning "proceed with caution." Men we spoke to, for the most part, say they are actually relieved when a woman clearly states what she wants. This takes the pressure off the man to be the "mind-reader," and allows both partners to plan and anticipate what will work for both.

Along with the fear of having to say no to others, one of the things that frequently stops people from venturing into the social arena is fear of rejection. Just about everyone we spoke with had at least one sad tale of putting their trust and expectations into a relationship, only to find the other person was not right for them or was not interested. In the frustration and hurt of such a situation, it is easy for people to blame themselves, the other person, or the situation. Let's take a look at Horror Story #4:

HORROR STORY 4

MAN MISPLACES HEART; DOESN'T SLEEP FOR DAYS.

At a dance, Jerry meets Jennifer, a young woman whom he is immediately enthralled with. They enjoy dancing together, and Jerry can't wait to see her again. He calls her and they make a date. They have an enjoyable evening and the chemistry seems to be there, but when the time comes to say "good night," Jerry gets a polite peck on the cheek and is sent on his way. After a few more pleasant but unromantic dates such as this one, Jerry says something like, "Hey Jennifer, what's going on? I thought you liked me."

Jennifer explains that it has been less than two months since she broke off a long-term relationship and she feels "numb" about getting involved with someone new. "I think our friendship is developing really well," she says, "and I'd like to keep it that way for now."

Jerry feels hurt and angry. HE hasn't been in a relationship in two years. HE wants a lover, not a platonic friendship. The rest of the evening is awkward at best, and Jerry goes home dejected. He also makes the following conclusions: 1) Women are deceptive; 2) He's not sexually attractive; 3) If he likes someone, she won't like him; and 4) He's never going to get what he wants.

ANTIDOTE TO HORROR STORY 4: IF YOU WANT TO DEVELOP CHEMISTRY, DO SOME SOCIAL STUDIES FIRST.

Think back (if it's not too painful) to the times you felt rejected. How many of these rejections now seem in the cold sober light of objectivity to be simply mismatches in social agenda? (Be honest.) Jerry made several near-fatal mistakes, and most of these involved not looking for matching social agendas, but instead making conclusions based on what he HOPED would be true. The first evening, he assumed the attraction was a romantic, sexual one. He never checked this out with Jennifer, either by asking a direct question or by asking her some general questions about her past relationships and what she was looking for now and in the future. Nor did Jennifer volunteer much information about herself, but then she wasn't the one who was going overboard with fantasies.

Jerry, when he did hear the bad news, made another series of faulty conclusions. Instead of seeing that there was simply a mismatch of agendas—that is, they each wanted different things at the present time—Jerry decided that Jennifer did not like him (even though she said she did!) and that he was unattractive. From here he made the ultimate leap of faithlessness to the conclusion that he will never find anyone! Many people assume they are being rejected, when the problem is simply a mismatch of Life Stage, Life Course, or Life-style.

KEY 12

"There is no such thing as rejection— only mismatches."

The kind of chemistry that lasts can develop only after both people have "qualified" the other person to see if their social agendas match. Mismatches can be avoided by first developing a social agenda, then by pursuing it through activities you enjoy and communicating it to others. The final—and most significant—step is checking it out to see whether your agendas really match those of the other person. This can be a process of trial and error, but as long as you keep in mind that (a) You have every right to want what you want, and (b) You probably will eventually find it, you can actually enjoy the game of finding matches. We hope the following story will illustrate.

GOLDILOCKS AND THE THREE VOLLEYBALL GAMES

Once upon a time in a medium-sized Midwestern town, there lived a young woman named Goldilocks, so named because her parents liked fairy tales. Now Goldilocks was a happy-go-lucky, energetic young woman, and the one thing in life she loved more than anything else was volleyball. She enjoyed playing the game skillfully and playing to win, but she also liked laughing and shouting and having fun with people on both teams. So she set out to find her Ideal Volleyball Game. She told her friends. She told her co-workers. She even stood outside of sporting goods stores waiting to pounce on the first person who walked out with a volleyball.

One day, she spied a woman with the name of a volleyball team on her T-shirt. The woman told Goldilocks she belonged to a team called the "Kamikaze Death Squad," and invited Goldilocks to a practice. Goldilocks showed up and found out these were SERIOUS volleyball players. The only time any of the players smiled was when they had smashed a ball down an opponent's throat. After being knocked flat by a vicious spike and stepped on by two of her own teammates, Goldilocks decided the Kamikaze Death Squad was not for her. "Too hard," she decided, and left.

The following Sunday, she was invited to a picnic. "Get ready for some volleyball," she was told. Eagerly, she prepared for a friendlier game than the last one had been. What she found was dozens of people on the court, as well as dogs, toddlers, and people who said things like, "I haven't played in seventeen years" and proceeded to prove it. "Why keep score?" one of the people said. "We'll just play until we feel like quitting."

Goldilocks felt like quitting then, and she did. "Too soft," she muttered, walking off the field. One of the people at the picnic caught up with her as she was leaving. "I see you enjoy playing volleyball and play well," he told her. "Why don't you come to our game next Friday night?"

"Well, I've been pretty discouraged," Goldilocks said. "I'm looking for a game where people play to win but are also there to have fun."

"Sounds like our game is just your style," the man said. "We have some good players and play pretty well, but we never get down on people for making mistakes. There's also a lot of laughing and shouting. After the game, we go out for a few beers. It's a great way to meet people. I think you'll like it."

She did. After a thoroughly enjoyable Friday night, Goldilocks promised to return the very next week. "This one is just right," she said smiling.

As the story illustrated, it may take some time to find a match but it is well worth the wait. Sometimes—as in the first two volleyball games—it is easy to see when there isn't a match. It's also easy to get discouraged. If you've found three potential dating partners that don't match, you may feel you will never find someone who is suitable. Be patient. Even if you do find a person or situation that seems to qualify, it may take a number of conversations over several meetings to see if there really is a match.

Gary's story is an excellent illustration of how a clearly developed social agenda, pursued with an eye toward finding a match, can pay off. "By the time I returned to graduate school a few years ago," Gary says, "I had decided to try to meet a woman I might be able to establish an ongoing relationship with. I had been involved in a number of unsatisfactory relationships with women and was feeling that I had been pursuing the wrong women for the wrong reasons.

"I thought school was a good opportunity to meet someone special enough to stay with for a while. This was the first time in my life that I felt I was serious about looking for someone, and was sure about what I wanted. My strategy—which seems ridiculous when I think about it now—consisted of numbers and probability. If you are a salesperson or entrepreneur, it makes sense that the more people you contact, the greater the probability of selling your product or ideas. I set my sights on meeting and getting to know as many women (ones I was really interested in) as was reasonably possible while I was in graduate school. When I say getting to know, I mean talking with them and trying to find out about who they really were. I had also decided not to get distracted by my sexual needs or my fantasy world which had, on occasion, gotten in my way in the past. I had, as a male, finally learned to say no to myself.

"I began having casual conversations in class with those women I was interested in knowing better. It seemed like no big deal. Then I moved to meeting women for coffee or lunch. I almost never got turned down. From these low-key encounters the other person and I were able to see if we were interested in going further. If we were, the next step was going for walks, to movies, and maybe dinner or a bar to hear music.

"As a result, I met the woman I now live with. I first saw her in a class where she smiled and seemed friendly. I was curious and wanted to talk to her that first day, but didn't. A few days later, we saw each other briefly at a small neighborhood grocery parking lot. We looked at each other, smiled, and went on. We eventually saw each other again in the library, and I asked her out for coffee as a break from studying.

"We began seeing each other more and I think we both were surprised to find we connected in some important ways. We eventually made an agreement not to date other people while we tested the waters with each other. Over the past three years, our relationship has evolved and we are still together."

Gary began his "quest" by knowing the qualities that he wanted, and with a firm intention that he was serious about finding it. He had the patience to go out and meet women, put his sexual needs second, and find out if first he could develop friendships. This enabled him to "find out who was home" more objectively than if he had first become sexually involved. He also invited the women he met to join him in safe, short-term activities such as a quick coffee or short walk. On the basis of mutual interest, the next step was to spend evenings together—and let things develop naturally.

It may seem cold and calculating to simply go for numbers, but it was the knowledge that if he met enough women he would find a match that kept Gary on track. Closely related to the fear of rejection is the belief that there aren't enough people out there who match your agenda. Unless you're in the market for a 6' 10" Buddhist tightrope walker, we think you're mistaken.

As you feel more comfortable in communicating clearly and gracefully what you want, you will find it easier to gently, firmly turn down those people and situations that don't match what you really want. Says Greta, "I never realized until recently how my fear of having to say no kept me in safe situations only. I now see that to find quality, I may have to deal with quantity, and I'm getting better at turning people down. Last week I was with a guy I had to say no to several times, and after about the third time, I actually began to feel comfortable saying no."

When you are aware of your own social agenda and curious and inquisitive about the social agendas of others, you will find yourself discovering matches naturally in the normal course of your conversations. Once there is a basic match of general outlook, lifestyle, interests, and desired outcomes, chemistry will have a better chance to develop. Remember that natural personal attraction is great, but, alone, it is no substitute for matching social agendas. Or, as one of the people we spoke with said, "Just because you enjoy dancing with someone doesn't mean you want to have seventeen kids together."

CHECKLIST FOR MATCHING SOCIAL AGENDAS

You will know you are successfully matching social agendas when:

1. There is a basic comfort and good feeling in your social situations.

2. You find your friendships and relationships tend to develop smoothly and at a comfortable pace.

3. Most of the people and situations in your life suit who YOU are and what YOU love to do.

4. You feel more in control of your social environment because you know beforehand the other person's social agenda and what the event will be like.

5. You feel a harmony in your relationships, a sense of trust, and mutual acceptance.

6. You rarely if ever get into sticky social situations because you've developed a nose for mismatches.

7. People enjoy conversations with you because you are genuinely curious about them.

8. People compliment you on how clearly you ask for what you want, and how politely you say no.

As with any new behavior, pursuing and communicating your social agenda will have to be practiced. It may feel awkward, uncomfortable, or difficult at first, and this is to be expected. But you will find it will become easier gradually, and as it does you will feel—and truly be—more in control of your social life.

Chapter 6

66The people you want to meet are out doing the things you like to do — here's how to find them99

At this point, you might be saying to yourself, "The idea that I can meet people doing what I love to do sounds good in theory, but will it really work for me?" Right now, you just don't know anyone who shares your interest in pet breeding, white water rafting, or foreign films. And you're not quite sure how to go about finding them.

Perhaps you're feeling just the slightest twinge of anxiety as you think about going to new places, trying new activities, meeting new people. You've thought about calling that new country club, signing up for the life drawing class, or going to the dance a friend told you about, but you are wondering, "How can I find out if this is for me—before I go?" You are reminded of the last time you tried something new and had a perfectly dreadful time. That was the time a friend invited you to a rock club. You went anticipating great dance music—and found yourself at a geological exhibit!

Or perhaps you are excited about pursuing your social agenda, but feel shy or uncomfortable about talking to people about it. Whenever you think of your social agenda, what comes to mind is an acquaintance of yours who interrogates everyone as if he is Mike Wallace from "60 Minutes": "So what do you enjoy doing? How long have you lived here? What sign are you? Do you believe the balance of payments deficit adversely affects the steel industry?" You want to be able to get information from people without being overbearing. But you're not sure how to do it.

In the next two chapters you will go on a mission to generate, investigate, and qualify as many options as you can so YOU decide where you're going to meet people rather than accept the first thing that comes along. You will learn where to find options, how to narrow those to the most suitable ones, and how to communicate your social agenda to others in such a way that they will be glad to help you. You'll learn that the "Sherlock Holmes" phase— where you are tracking down the places and activities where you can meet the people you want to meet—is in itself an excellent way to meet people!

KEY 13

"Whatever your interests are, there are literally thousands of people out there who'd love to meet you!"

On a grassy hill just outside Gettysburg, Pennsylvania, dozens of men and women dressed in clothes from the 1860s take their places. A gun is fired and the battle begins. Within the hour, many blue- and grey-clad men lie strewn along the battleground, red stains seeping through their uniforms. Women circulate to help the wounded, and other people take photographs. After the mock battle, dinner is served. Everyone has a jolly time, and before getting in their cars to drive home, they make plans to be at the next "battle."

Each year, hundreds if not thousands of people get together to relive battles, enjoy Croatian folk dances, swap tall tales, discuss science fiction and dress up like their favorite characters, swim in 33 degree water, or watch birds. Others organize or participate in medieval festivals, jump from airplanes, learn how to survive in the mountains, or spend two weeks at a baseball fantasy camp. No matter what it is you enjoy doing, you are likely to find others who enjoy that same activity. Don't take our word for it—go to the library and look through the *Encyclopedia of Associations*. There you will find everything from the American Association of Aardvark Aficionados to the National Nudist Council, to DENSA, the "dull people's answer to MENSA." If your tastes run to more conventional pursuits—like chorale singing, bowling, co-ed softball, art appreciation—there are very likely organizations and networks in your own community where you can meet others with the same bent.

We aren't suggesting that you must join an organization to meet people with similar interests—far from it. But you do have many more options than you think, no matter what you enjoy doing. Why are options so important? Let's say you are looking forward to Saturday night. You have only one friend in town, and this friend loves to go to the movies on Saturday night. Let's say there's just one movie theater in town. Not only will that narrow your choices of activities for Saturday evening, it will also narrow your choices of movies. It won't matter whether you've already seen *The Mark of Zorro* fourteen times. If it's the only game in town, that's where you'll be.

This is only a slight exaggeration of what most people face. As the cliché goes, we are creatures of habit. We tend to go to the same restaurants and order the same few dishes, go to the same night spots, spend time with the same people. Often we realize we no longer enjoy these habits or activities, but, we say, what else is there to do? Remember the tale of "Goldilocks and the Three Volleyball Games" from the last chapter? If Goldilocks believed that volleyball game 1 or volleyball game 2 were the only games in town, she never would have found volleyball game 3—the one that worked for her. Having options also helps you feel better while you are in the process of doing your detective work. The more ways you have of getting what you want, the more comfortable and confident you will feel—and the less you will have to rely on any one choice.

Yes, generating options takes effort—but it can be fun. Yes, it can sometimes be a hassle choosing from several options, especially if you are not familiar with any of them. Yes, it can be time-consuming to make phone calls, talk to people about places you are considering going to, making "on site" inspections. But think of how much time you've spent doing what you didn't enjoy, NOT meeting the people you wanted to meet, only because you had NOTHING BETTER TO DO. Think of all the boring and/or unpleasant evenings you have endured, and consider that you could have avoided many unsatisfying hours with just a few hours of well-spent planning time.

Once you have decided to spend your time planning and investigating rather than accepting and enduring, you will never again want to let circumstance determine what you do. And you will be meeting more interesting people and having more fun than you ever imagined possible. But YOU must make the decision. The rest of this chapter will help you carry out your plan—and have fun doing it.

KEY 14

"When you look before you leap, you can choose where you land."

Of course, generating options is just the first step. Options in and of themselves are no guarantee against boring or unpleasant times. The confusion of having too many options can be as intimidating and frustrating as having too few. And even with just a few options, how do you know which are most likely to be what you're looking for? You have to QUALIFY the options. So before we go any further with creating options, let's look at how to qualify them. That way, you'll be able to do some of the selecting while you are generating options, and the choices you do come up with will be more likely to suit you.

You qualify the options by seeing how they stack up against what is most important to you. Let's say you wanted to buy a home. You make a list of all the things you want, and these might include:

spacious	has parking available
light and airy	must have space for office
finished basement	fireplace

near work	out in the country
reasonable price	low taxes
not much repair to do	nothing to maintain
investment opportunity	at least five rooms

You might then prioritize the list in order of importance. For example, money might be the most important issue for you. Therefore, purchase price might come first. Or else comfort or convenience might be the top criterion for you. So on that basis, you might choose a place in the country, a luxurious setting, nearby parking, and so on. Style or design might be most important to you, so you might choose a home with a fireplace or an older home or a modern apartment or whatever. But in each case, YOU are deciding what is most important to YOU, and you are choosing on that basis.

Choosing the places you will go to meet people is a similar process. Like your home, the activities and places you choose are ones you will have to live with. They need to be environments that suit you, where you will be comfortable, and of course, where you will be able to meet the people you want to meet. Therefore, as you consider places and activities, you might want to ask the following questions:

- Can I do what I love to do there?
- Is it likely to be fun?
- Does it appeal to me?
- Am I likely to meet the people I want to meet?
- Does it fit my other personal standards (i.e., likes and dislikes)?
- Can I be myself in the situation?

Then decide which of these criteria are most important to you. Perhaps in the past you have been uncomfortable in new situations meeting people. So you might choose comfort and being able to be yourself as your most important criteria. It may be important that you meet certain kinds of people (e.g., nonsmokers, college educated, wealthy, religious, nonconformist, etc.), so you might make that your top criteria. Or, if you really want to have fun meeting people, that might be your priority. And so on. Remember that YOU are the expert when it comes to what is best for you.

Let's look at Margaret, who loves to go dancing. She LIKES popular dance music, neatly dressed men, good conversation, space to dance. She DISLIKES cigarette smoke, drunks, crowded spaces, heavy metal music, overbearing men. She knows that if she has people to dance with and the music is right, she will have fun. She wants to meet single men over thirty who are financially secure, although not seeking to impress with their wealth. And she wants to dance in a place with a friendly atmosphere. She decided that the most important criterion for her is the people—that they're intelligent and playful—the kind of people she wants to meet. Next comes the music, because if she doesn't like the music, she won't dance. If the people and music are right, she might be willing to tolerate a small dance floor, smoke, and crowds. Keeping this in mind, she is ready to begin her investigation.

Of course, she realizes that the best way to know what is for her is to go there and see, hear, and get a feel for what it is like. But in her town, there are no less than thirty dance spots. Margaret is busy with work and other commitments, and wants to spend her precious leisure time well. Perhaps, she thinks, she can qualify—and disqualify—some without actually going there. So she begins with her friends, and asks, "Where do you like to go to dance?" She is careful to first find out whether her friends' standards and criteria match her own. A friend who enjoys punk rock, for example, might have a different idea of where the best dance spot is. She then asks the friend to describe in detail what the place is like. Questions may include: What do you like about the place? What don't you like? What is the music like? Is it loud? What are the people like? How do they dress? Is it crowded? Smoky? How big is the dance floor? Have you met any people there? Do you like those you've met? Margaret has her friend describe the place using all the senses: What does it look like? How does it sound? How does it feel to be there?

As Margaret talks with her friends, she is able to rule out two places—a country-western bar, and a place where all the college kids hang out and dance. She has two options she is still considering—an elegant disco, and a dance spot located in a downtown hotel. Talking with friends had still another benefit. In the course of her conversation, she has found several "allies" with similar criteria who want to go with her to check these places out.

But she is still not satisfied with just two possibilities. So she goes to the Yellow Pages and looks under "bars" and "clubs." Here she immediately rules out dozens of places where there is no dancing. She also finds a couple of places that seem like possibilities—an "oldies" dance spot, and a new bar which advertises "dance to top-40 music." She makes a note to ask friends and acquaintances about these places, and if necessary to call them herself. She also looks in the community calendar in the local newspaper to see which bands are playing where this weekend. Here she finds something really intriguing—the local chapter of the American Lung Association is holding its monthly "Butt Kickers' Ball," which she discovers is a smokeless dance to raise money for research. She marks this down as a definite possibility, and smiles as she realizes that she never would have heard of it if she hadn't looked in the community calendar.

So where do you begin generating and selecting YOUR options? The answer is, wherever it is easiest for YOU. Some people prefer to begin by talking to their friends and acquaintances. Others might begin with activities. Some might go directly to the Yellow Pages or *Encyclopedia of Associations* to begin their sleuthing. And there are those who will do all three. Whichever strategy you employ, you are looking for activities, groups, and settings that will be fun, that will allow you to do what you love to do, and will provide the opportunity to meet the people you want to meet. We urge you to be RELENTLESS in generating lots of choices for yourself rather than settling for one or two "also-ran" situations. Above all, remember that the investigation process can be an easy, enjoyable way to meet new people, find out which of your acquaintances share your social agenda, and help each other find new social activities networks.

KEY 15

" Your friends and acquaintances are an excellent resource for finding social activities networks. "

"Back when I was a junior at George Washington University," says Elaine, thirty-two, "I was sharing an apartment with my friend Gloria, whom I met when we were in the same freshman dorm. She took me to a party sponsored by her art club and introduced me to Chuck. Chuck and I became friends and stayed in contact over the next few years while he traveled around the country working with a number of museums. Eventually, we both ended up in Illinois, but in different towns. So he invited me to visit him in Chicago for a weekend, and took me to a gallery opening where I met Jeff. He and I hit it off immediately. Jeff and I went out for quite a while, and we are still very close friends. What I concluded from all this was we tend to gravitate towards others with similar interests, tastes, and ideas of how to enjoy life. These types of social networks are an ideal way to meet people."

Over and over again in our interviews, we heard stories like this one—people meeting people they like through shared activities with people they already know. Chances are you have one or many stories like this one. All of us have been part of a social network, whether it was our class at school, our Little League team, Boy Scout or Girl Scout troop, church group, fraternity, sorority, co-workers, bowling team, the people we go to parties with, and so forth. Social networks can be as formal as a professional association, as informal as kids break-dancing on the streets. They can revolve around common interests, professional activity, family, play, or just friends out to have a good time. The social networks we're concerned with here have a definite focus on fun activities. You can find these social activities networks through your friends—and you can find new friends through these social activities networks. More often than not, when you find people who share common interests, these people may in turn lead you to other friends and activities.

BEGIN WITH THE PEOPLE YOU KNOW AND LIKE AND RADIATE OUTWARD

Make a list of the people you like. They can be close friends, family members, acquaintances, people you just say "hello" to on the street. If you have found something attractive or likeable about them, they may be able to expand your social activities network. In our interviews and workshops, a word that comes up over and over again is "likeable." People who are likeable tend to know a lot of other people—people they can introduce you to. Now go through your list of people and note which of them are the easiest to approach, which are a bit more difficult to approach, and which are most difficult to approach. Unless you like doing things the hard way, you will be approaching the easiest first!

Usually, the easiest place to begin is with the people you know the best. Particularly if you are not in the habit of networking, begin with the people you are most comfortable with. Find out what THEY love to do. You might discover an activity you would also enjoy. And you might find a mutual interest you didn't know you shared. Also, find out about others they know who enjoy what you do. Ask them if it's okay to mention their name when you call these people.

Tactfully approach the people at work, the people you carpool with, the people you say hello to each day, and find out what excites them. If they seem interested, tell them what you love to do. You may find yourself on your way to making a new friend. Ask the people in one social group (e.g., your soccer team) if they might be interested in another activity you like (e.g., sailing).

Suppose you are looking for a place to play tennis where you can meet other people who play at your level and whom you might want to have as friends. You might begin by letting your friends know what you are looking for and enlisting their help. When you feel comfortable with people, it's relatively easy to bring up your social agenda in the natural flow of conversation. You might begin a conversation on the subject something like this: "You know, I've been thinking lately that I miss playing tennis, and I'd like to start playing regularly again. Not only is it fun, but it could be an excellent way to meet people." If you know your friends play tennis, you might ask them to play with you, or else ask where they play and who else they know who plays. Let them know as specifically as possible what you are looking for. Use stories and examples from your past experience to give friends a specific idea of what you're looking for.

You might approach a good friend from work—someone you haven't socialized with much. Here, you might ask, "Say, I was wondering, do you play tennis?" If the person does play, you have found a potential partner. If not, he or she might have some friends who play. The idea is to have fun finding out—and to let the other person know you are, in turn, open to helping them meet people. You might say, "You know, I really like it when I can help people find a social circle or activity they'll enjoy. If you let me know what you like to do, I'll be on the look-out." Being a "fun detective" of this sort is an excellent way to discover new options, meet people, and make friends. But before you offer your services make sure you have your friend's permission.

Sometimes people feel uncomfortable approaching friends and acquaintances with an agenda, and this is understandable. People generally want to be treated like people, not data banks. On the other hand, if you approach people in a considerate, respectful, and appreciative way, they will enjoy being helpful.

MAKE IT A HABIT TO FIND OUT
WHAT PEOPLE LOVE TO DO

Getting people to talk about what really turns them on—provided they're willing to—is a great way to build rapport. Invariably people will light up, become more animated, and speak in more excited tones when they are talking about something they love to do. At a party recently we noticed a man and a woman talking about a mutual love, travel. Although they had never met before, they were standing on common ground. As each relayed an experience, their rapport intensified. They unconsciously moved closer together and touched each other more frequently. After a while, two other people who had not done much traveling approached and joined the conversation. Soon the two travelers grew even closer together as they realized they shared feelings and experiences the two nontravelers couldn't possibly understand.

Pursuing your agenda will not only put you in touch immediately with what you have in common with other people, but it might get you excited about trying an activity you always wanted to try. As you meet people you like through your social activity networks—be it jazzercize or playing bridge or going to discussion groups—there's an opportunity to find out if you have any other loves in common. Are you playing on a softball team? Find out if anyone there wants to go to the "Fitness Expo" that's going on downtown. Hanging out with the "happy hour" crowd after work? Maybe someone wants to go to the Marx Brothers festival on Saturday evening. The one sure way to find out what other people are interested in is to ask.

You can also survey people you meet at work or strangers you meet at parties about their interests and social agendas. Marla took a new job in a new town, and knew virtually no one. At work, however, she noticed another woman who appeared to be single and fun. One day, she approached the other woman at the water cooler and suggested they go out for a drink after work. They found they had similar interests—enjoyment of the outdoors—and social agendas—meeting men they would like to go out with. So together they went to the ski club in town. They had a great time, and joined that night. Says Marla, "It really helped to have someone to share my feelings with. And when it came to meeting-people ideas, two heads were better than one. Without a friend, I don't know if I would have had the courage to walk into this new social setting."

Having a "mission" to find out as much as you can about

others serves at least two purposes. First, it allows you to find common ground almost immediately. Second, you become less self-conscious and self-absorbed when you focus your attention on getting to know someone else. Most people enjoy having someone genuinely interested in them. In playing Sherlock Holmes or Nancy Drew, however, be sure and attune yourself to the other person's feelings. First of all, do they want to participate? Are your questions gentle, or overly probing? Are you giving the other person the spotlight— or putting them on the spot? Are you letting them know you are genuinely interested, or do you come across as a census taker?

Some of the questions you can ask to elicit people's social agendas and interests are: What else do you do for fun? What was your most enjoyable time ever? What was your craziest or most unusual people-meeting situation? What do you like most about doing such-and-such? To loosen people up a bit, make sure the sharing is mutual. Offer something about yourself, about what turns YOU on. By letting other people know what you want, you are recruiting them into your social quest. Leslie is a good example of this. With her husband and her two small children, Leslie moved to a new town where she knew no one. Since she's home most of the day, she felt particularly isolated. She wanted to meet other mothers of small children—to share ideas with, to share babysitting, to chat with, to joke with. One of her interests is natural childbirth and breastfeeding, so she talked to a midwife friend of hers back home who suggested she contact La Leche League, an organization sharing information on breastfeeding. Leslie ended up volunteering to answer the telephones and made several new friends, used her skills as an organizer and communicator, and promoted an idea she supports.

Dave was looking for people to play music with so he told everyone he knew. A week later, one of his housemates came home and said the next door neighbors were going to have a music-making party. Dave went to the party, hit it off with the musicians, and was promised an invitation to their next get-together the following month. Then a guy at work told him of a group of guitarists that got together every Wednesday evening. Dave went once and decided to make it a regular thing. Before the end of his first year in town, Dave was picking and choosing from a wide variety of musicians, and had even been asked to play in a band.

Communicating your social agenda can be a fruitful— and highly enjoyable—mission. At parties, at work, on the bus, the people who are most successful at meeting people are always curious about other people. Practice telling people your social agenda, and begin with yourself. Stand in front of the mirror and tell yourself what you are looking for. How does it sound to you? Do you sound convincing? Doubtful? Enthusiastic? Bored? As soon as you feel comfortable with your social agenda and how it sounds, begin to share it with your close friends. Have them respond to it and see if it comes across in the way you intended. The more you tell others what you want, the more comfortable it will feel.

LEARN TO GET SPECIFIC INFORMATION TACTFULLY

First, let's look at how NOT to do it. Our friend Sue received a phone call recently from a woman she had met just briefly who was looking for work. Without really asking permission, the woman began asking her questions about how she runs her business. Sue brought the conversation to an end as soon as she could. Talking about the experience afterward, she said, "I don't really mind offering help to people—if they ask the right way. First of all, she called while I was fixing dinner. She didn't ask if it was a good time. She just went right ahead with her questions. She didn't stop to find out what I needed, and didn't tell me what was in it for me. It felt too one-sided, and I began to resent her aggressiveness. If only we had established some kind of rapport, I would have helped her."

The caller made several glaring errors, and as a result failed to get the information she wanted. First, she failed to get permission. She just assumed Sue was willing to talk with her at that time. Second, she failed to establish rapport. That is, she didn't create common ground so that Sue trusted her. As a result, Sue felt ripped off. Finally, she did not find out what Sue wanted, which further fueled Sue's suspicion that this was an all-give, no-get situation. Although it may be difficult at first to get used to calling strangers on the phone, it is a skill that is worth developing—and it usually turns out to be much easier than you would imagine—provided you follow these simple rules.

1. GET PERMISSION. When calling people you've never met, introduce yourself, tell them how you got their name and briefly outline what it is you want from them. Listen carefully for whether they are available, interested, and willing to talk. As soon as you have introduced yourself, find out if this is a good time to call. If it isn't, ask, "What would be a better time for you?" Be specific about how much time this is likely to take: Can I talk to you for a few minutes? Do you have ten minutes to spend with me on the phone? And so on. A telephone call gives you entry into a private home. Therefore, don't walk in until you are invited. No matter how well you know the people, make sure your timing is right.

2. ESTABLISH RAPPORT.   People who have a natural knack for making contact and making friends know it's essential to establish some common ground before proceeding with a discussion. Rapport doesn't happen by magic—it's something you can learn. One of the easiest ways to establish a common base with a new person on the phone is through reference. "Hello, my name is George Smith. Bart Jones suggested I call you." The person then can associate you with someone already known, and begin to trust you. Of course, don't say Bart Jones suggested you call unless he really did! Let the person know immediately how you got his or her name. Was it a mutual friend or acquaintance? A mailing list? An ad? This will give the person a reference point, and be the first step toward establishing rapport.

One of the best ways to establish rapport, of course, is by talking about the activity you mutually enjoy. "One of the things I really enjoy," Linda told us, "is cooking and eating exotic food. I decided that I wanted to form a little group that would get together monthly and cook and enjoy these foods. Through a friend at work, I found out that another of our co-workers was interested in the same thing. I was a little reluctant to call him at first, but I got up my courage and did it anyway. As soon as I told him what I was calling about, he got really excited and we talked nonstop for half an hour. Not only did he bring four of his friends with him, but he insisted on inviting me over for dinner next time."

Not every conversation will be as fruitful as Linda's. But if you are polite and sensitive to the other person, there's a good chance he or she will be friendly and helpful. The key to maintaining rapport once you have it is to listen carefully to the other person. Is she enthusiastic? Is he getting bored or restless? Is she getting what she wants? A successful hospital administrator told us, "Whenever I meet someone I am doing business with, I always make sure I find out what he needs. Then I make sure that if it's in my power, I give it to him. Often, I find that he ends up calling to ask what HE can do for ME."

After you've established rapport and the conversation is moving along well, be sure you get the information you called to get! Let's say a friend told you about a group that gets together every Friday evening to play *Trivial Pursuit*. You might say, "I get really excited about going out when I have a clear idea of what the event is going to be like. So the more you can tell me about it, the more I will look forward to it." And then you can ask: Who is likely to be there? What do you enjoy about these people? What do you think I will particularly enjoy about the evening? What is the setting like? Will there be any food served? And so on.

3. MAKE SURE YOU OFFER AS WELL AS ASK.   If you're calling someone for information, let her know early on in the conversation how you can help HER. If you are calling because a mutual friend suggested she might want to play handball, you can offer to share everything you learn about good places to play. If you are calling a graphic artist because you are a copy writer looking for work, you can suggest turning the artist on to any contacts you find. Whatever your purpose in calling, be sure the other person feels benefited by the conversation. Offer your resources and your assistance. If the other person benefits, chances are you will, too. And who knows? You might make a new friend!

We know someone who enjoys social networking so much that she keeps a special address book with "favorite activities" next to the person's name. That way, if she comes across another person who enjoys the same thing, she calls her friend and gives him or her the other person's name. We're not necessarily recommending that you do this, although our friend meets a lot of people who call her when they are looking for apartments, roommates, work, or just want to know where the parties are.

4. ENJOY YOURSELF!   Remember that social networking is part of the people-meeting process—so enjoy it! Each phone call, each new person you talk with, each new activity or lead you get, is an adventure. The next phone call you make may change your life. The next person you meet may become your best friend. The next activity you go to may be the best time you've ever had. Approach each contact with a sense of adventure and enthusiasm, and you'll find you'll have as much fun looking as doing.

5. ACKNOWLEDGE AND APPRECIATE THE PEOPLE WHO HELP YOU.   Think about the last time you received a note of thanks, and remember how it felt. Make a habit of thanking people, either by phone, by mail, or in person when they help you find out about an activity or meet someone. You will find they are more likely to be of help in the future—and you might nurture a budding friendship.

No matter what your social agenda is, make it a priority to cultivate your social activities networks. Particularly if you are new in an area or in a new life situation, the networks you are involved in can be your lifeline to good times—and meeting more of the people you want to meet. A thriving social activities network means more options, it means coming in contact with more people who share your interests and values—and it means higher quality friendships.

In the next chapter you'll discover how to meet people through activities, organizations, dating services, singles' ads, and through events and situations you and your friends design. All of these methods can be used to build your social activities networks.

Chapter 7

"Expanding your social activities network"

Certainly social networks are a great way to meet people. But suppose you don't have a social network or you're dissatisfied with the networks you're in? What if you're new in town? Suppose none of your friends or acquaintances know anything about skydiving, amateur theater, or archeological digs? If that's your situation, the answer is to go directly to the activity you enjoy or think you might enjoy. Once again, the challenge is to first generate as many options as you need to choose from, and then make an informed choice based on what suits you best.

DECIDE WHAT YOU'RE LOOKING FOR

As we said in Chapter Five, the more you know about what you want, the more likely you are to find it. If you keep ending up at places that just don't seem right for you, you probably need to do this step a bit more thoroughly. Look at your social agenda carefully. Ask yourself, does this state clearly what I am looking for? What are your other criteria? Let's say you're looking for a place to play racquetball. What kind of people are you looking for to play with? What are their attitudes? Skill levels? Do you want male or female partners? What would you like the environment to be like? Elegant? Homey? The people you play with—should they be single? Married? Professionals? Students? The more you know at this stage, the easier it will be to rule out what you don't want. For example, if you want to play with singles, you might eliminate the club that emphasizes family packages. You want the atmosphere to be casual, the price reasonable. Then you can rule out the club that advertises a string quartet and champagne in the locker room. As you make your "rules," be aware that people sometimes make the rules so stringent that they automatically rule out just about everything. So ask yourself, am I being realistic? Or am I sabotaging my search for options by setting impossible standards?

GATHER YOUR RESOURCES

We have found that when people believe there is a lack of opportunities to meet people, there is really just a lack of knowledge as to where to find these opportunities. Therefore, we suggest that you familiarize yourself with the myriad of resources out there just waiting to be used. The resources that are most useful in meeting people include: the Yellow Pages, classified and display advertising, community calendars, bulletin boards, and the library.

THE YELLOW PAGES   Perhaps the most valuable— and accessible—resource directory you have is the Yellow Pages sitting near your telephone. In it you will find a listing for just about every organization, recreational facility, and activity imaginable. It is the first place you should look, because it is the most complete local directory, and because looking through the listings and categories can spur your imagination and present you with options you didn't know you had.

Pat, married and the mother of two small children, had been a track star in high school. Now that her children were attending preschool, she was ready to resume a career in the fitness field. She didn't know where to begin, so she started with the Yellow Pages. First, she noted all the health and fitness clubs and began calling them. Then she looked under "shoes" and found several stores specializing in running shoes. At that point, she decided to approach those stores for a sales position since she knew so much about running. She also looked under physicians, chiropractors, and physical therapists, and found at least two chiropractors and physical therapists who specialized in sports-related injuries. With just an afternoon's work, she had a list of fifteen resources that might possibly lead to jobs. Not only did she finally end up with a job in the fitness field, but she expanded her network and made a few new friends in the process.

CLASSIFIED AND DISPLAY ADVERTISING

Advertisements, like Yellow Pages listings, are great resources because the persons or organizations who placed the ad are actively looking for someone—and it might be you they are looking for. Are you interested in dancing? Concerts? Theater? Look at the ads in the entertainment section of your newspaper! Are you interested in fitness? Look at the sports pages. Business seminars? Look in the business section.

Bob, a business consultant, wanted to pursue an interest in photography. While looking through his local newspaper, he noticed that the city's community education program was offering a photography class. "I took the class," he recalls, "and made an entirely new group of friends just because of that one ad. I had so much fun that I went back and took other classes in things I'd always wanted to do like creative writing and theater playshop. For me, it was a very easy way to meet interesting, active people—and a lot more satisfying than the singles' scene."

Many of the people we spoke with reported that they had met people in classes and workshops. In most towns, the "Y", local community colleges, and the community education departments offer a wide variety of noncredit classes for adults wishing to pursue their interests in a leisurely, social setting. In one town, for example, there is a thriving, independent "learning network" that offers classes in such areas as photography, camping, creative writing, foreign languages, meditation, effective communication, computer skills, ethnic cooking, and more. Whatever classes you choose, though, make sure it's something you're really interested in, or at least interested enough to give it a try. Taking a class as a thinly veiled excuse to meet people can be spotted a mile away. A friend of ours who teaches aerobic dance reports, "We sometimes have men take our classes—which is great—but every now and then a guy shows up with no interest in exercise at all. He's just there to watch. It's a big turn-off to all the others in the class who are genuinely interested in learning."

Don was new in town and was casually thumbing through the newspaper classifieds when he saw an ad for a "Men's Group." Since he was looking for men friends and liked the idea of a discussion group, he called. The group itself was not to his liking, but he did meet a man who became his best friend in town. His friend introduced him to his circle of friends, they played on the same softball team, and even played music together. What began with an ad in the paper ended with a social network.

COMMUNITY CALENDARS   Just about every newspaper, city magazine, newsletter, or specialty publication has a calendar of events. Radio stations, universities, large corporations, and libraries have calendars as well. The beauty of community calendars is that they give you options you can do today, tomorrow, this week, this month. And they might spur your imagination and let you know about an option you might never have thought of.

While looking through a newspaper calendar, Judy noticed there was a workshop on "Drawing on the Right Side of Your Brain" coming up on the weekend. Although she had never thought of herself as an artist, the calendar item said anyone could do it. Says Judy, "I was feeling bored and dissatisfied with what I was doing. It was a combination of not being around the right kind of people, and getting in a rut at work. Anyway, I took a chance and went to this workshop and had a blast. I met three or four people I now see regularly, and we really have fun together. And they have helped me find a new group of friends, who have in turn encouraged me to go back to school in a field that suits me better. I was really ready for a change. I'm glad I saw that ad when I did."

BULLETIN BOARDS   Bulletin boards are really a combination of ads and calendars. The best bulletin boards are the most specific ones—the ones focusing on entertainment or health or personal growth or travel opportunities. Says Pamela, a psychotherapist who is interested in personal growth, "Whenever I visit a new city, the way I find the people I want to meet is through bulletin boards. I usually will make a stop at a health food store, because they tend to have bulletin boards related to all areas of growth. There I can find a drop-in yoga class listed, or a lecture, or even a business card. If I find a business card that intrigues me I'll call the person. Sometimes we really hit it off, and I've made several friends that way." Bulletin boards are an excellent way to tap into social activities networks.

THE LIBRARY   The best thing about the library is that it has resources and directories you didn't know existed. The next best thing about the library is the trained personnel who are paid to help you find those resources! The librarians we spoke to get a kick out of helping people. Because they are constantly receiving flyers, clipping articles, reading through newsletters, they are natural networkers who know what's going on in the community. Library bulletin boards are generally crammed with flyers on local activities, particularly free or nonprofit events. Librarians can also steer you to local and national publications geared toward some specific activity. Our local librarian showed us that fascinating directory, *The Encyclopedia of Associations,* which we mentioned in the last chapter. It lists just about every club and organization that exists. If you are not yet convinced that there is something for everyone, take a journey through this book. Here you will find organizations for every ethnic and social group imaginable as well as model train hobbyists, hog callers, tellers of tall tales, believers in a flat earth, on and on. Carl, who was interested in science fiction, had heard that there were periodic conferences for science fiction aficionados where they could meet their favorite authors, dress up like their favorite characters, and of course, meet new friends. He tried the Yellow Pages, community calendar, classified ads, but could find nothing. So he went to his local librarian, who suggested he look in the *Encyclopedia of Associations.* There he found a national organization that put on these conferences, and he quickly fired off a letter. A week later he received a packet in the mail with details on the next conference, information on how to join the organization, and the address of the closest chapter.

For those people who enjoy sleuth work, gathering information in this way can be fun and exciting. Discovery, adventure—and of course, new friends—lurk behind every turn. After the research phase, you should have at least five, maybe more, options in the form of places, organizations, activities that appear to match your social agenda. The next step will be to narrow these options. Before moving on to that stage, ask yourself these questions: Am I satisfied that I have enough options to choose from? Do any of these options seem particularly exciting to me? Can any be ruled out immediately? Keep in mind that people sometimes get stuck at the option-gathering phase and never get around to following up on any of them. If you have been researching for two months, but haven't gotten around to actually checking any of your options out, we suggest you move on to the next section immediately!

NARROWING YOUR OPTIONS

If you are like most people, you work forty or more hours a week. Your free time is limited, so you want to spend it wisely. It can be time-consuming to follow up each option in person, particularly when it might mean devoting an entire evening or weekend even to finding out if it's for you. Chances are you have already ruled out a number of options just on the basis of the written material you have seen. There are some that seem to be definite "doers," and still others are possibilities, but you simply don't know much about them. The telephone is your best friend when it comes to narrowing your options to the ones that best match who you are and what you are looking for.

TIPS FOR SELECTING
YOUR OPTIMAL OPTIONS

1. Remind yourself of your criteria. Make two lists—"Option Makers" and "Option Breakers." Under the Option Makers list, write all the things that would attract you to a place, group, or activity. For Margaret, the woman we mentioned in Chapter Six who was looking for the right place to go dancing, Option Makers would include: dance music she enjoys, a young professional crowd, people who like to have fun, a spacious dance floor, and good ventilation. Under the Option Breakers list, write everything you can think of that would cause you to rule out an option immediately. Margaret's Option Breakers might include: not her style of dance music, a crowd that was too young (or old), cramped space, too smoky. As you talk to people about prospective activities, refer to these lists frequently.

2. Know what it is you want to find out. Most busy people find that if they make notes before telephone conversations, they cover everything efficiently. So before calling, write out a list of questions. At the top of the page, list the things you already know about the place. Then list what you would like to know. If, for example, you were looking for a racquetball club, you might want to ask: How much does it cost to belong? Are there any additional costs? Who belongs? What are the facilities like? And so on.

3. Make sure you are talking to someone who knows what he is talking about. If you want more in-depth information, don't hesitate to ask for someone who can tell you what you want to know. Particularly if this is a group seeking new members or customers, they should be more than willing to give you this information. If not, consider it a red flag.

4. Make sure you get as complete a picture as possible. When you call, ask the person to describe the activity in detail. If you are considering going on a bike tour, you might ask: Who is likely to go along on this trip? What are their ages, life-styles, other interests? How long is the trip? How vigorous is the bicycling? What other social activities are planned? If you hang up the phone and you can't imagine what it would be like to go to the place, you definitely need more information.

5. Ask for references. Ask to speak to satisfied clients, customers, or members so that you can get a better idea if this is for you. Many organizations and businesses will gladly do this. If they won't, find out why. When you speak with the references, apply the rules of asking permission, establishing rapport, and benefiting them we discussed in the last chapter. As much as possible, get them to describe their experience in detail. The more you know about an organization, place, or activity, the easier it will be for you to decide whether it's for you.

6. Run each option past your criteria. Earlier in this chapter, we talked about prioritizing your criteria for people-meeting situations. For each option, look at your most important criteria and see how they measure up. Let's look at Margaret again, the woman who was looking for places to dance. Her criteria were, in order of importance:

- The people are fun-loving, mature, and considerate.
- The music is current and danceable.
- There is ample space to dance.
- It is not too smoky.
- There are few or no obnoxious drunks.

Margaret found it was easiest to find out the age of the crowd, the kind of music, and the size of the dance floor just by calling the places on the phone. A few of the people she spoke with were quite helpful and gave her more information. The places she didn't rule out immediately she divided into two groups: Have Enough Information, and Need More Information. Those she had enough information about, she divided into two categories: Definite Doers, and Maybes. The Definite Doers automatically went to the top of her "to do" list, and she made plans to check these out in person as soon as possible. The Maybes became her back-up options. Even though she was quite excited about her Definite Doers, she knew it was important to keep on generating options. So she made an agreement with herself to find out more about those options in her Need More Information category—and to keep finding even more good choices. A good rule of thumb is: never have fewer than three good options for each activity you want to pursue. If you find yourself feeling panicky, anxious, frustrated, cynical, or trapped, you may be suffering from the Too-Few-Choices Syndrome. Fortunately, there is an antidote—discover three new options daily. Repeat until symptoms vanish.

Before we move on to the final two sections of this chapter, which cover the very formal ways of expanding your social activities network (dating services, singles' organizations, and personals ads) and the very informal (fun events you plan with your friends), let's look at how Jane selected and qualified her people-meeting options. Unlike the people who enjoy dancing, group sports, workshops, and other naturally social events, Jane's interest in writing and literature presented her with a bit of a challenge. How could she turn these solitary pursuits into social pursuits? She decided to begin with her social agenda. A lively, witty woman of twenty-seven, Jane was perfectly satisfied with her job as a salesperson for a computer software firm, but was not satisfied with the people she met through her job. "I wanted to meet people who were a little more intellectual," she says, "who love to discuss 'great ideas' but who aren't stuffy. When I thought back to the terrific discussions I had with friends during my college days, I really missed those kinds of people. The men I was meeting were okay, but I wanted to meet more men who could really appreciate and support the clever writer and literary critic in me."

Jane began her resource gathering by communicating her social agenda to friends, particularly those who seemed to share her interests in intellectual pursuits. "I have one friend who is really great at coming up with unusual ideas," she says. "So I invited her out to lunch, told her what I was looking for, and suggested that we brainstorm how I could meet people through reading and writing. We had a lot of laughs as we came up with a number of hilarious and outrageous ideas. Ironically enough, one of the most outrageous ideas—that I do a 'book beat' type TV show locally—turned out to be one that I followed up on." She also asked other friends for ideas on where book lovers were likely to be. After a week, she had a general list of possible settings including libraries, bookstores, publishing houses, writer's classes and organizations, literature classes, and author's lectures at a nearby university. She also was considering freelance writing for magazines and newspapers, and possibly being involved in a TV show.

With these general categories in mind, Jane set out to find specific situations. Her first step was the Yellow Pages, where she found twenty or so new and used book stores in the area, located the community education departments in her locale, and found at least one writers' association. She next went and talked to the librarian at her local library, who told her they regularly held "Booked for Lunch" lectures with local authors and writers. The librarian also directed Jane to the bulletin board, where she found notices for a literary lecture series in a nearby city, and an announcement for a writer's workshop several hundred miles away. Later that week, she called the community education departments and the local university, and found out that there were classes available in contemporary literature (the kind she was interested in) and creative writing. Meanwhile, she was looking through the local newspaper when she saw an announcement asking for people who were interested in doing their own TV shows for the public access cable channel. She made a note of this as well, remembering her brainstorming session with her friend.

"All of a sudden there were all these possibilities," Jane recalls. "For the first time since college, I was really excited about the prospect of meeting interesting people." Before setting out to find specific information about these options, Jane decided to review her criteria for the ideal setting:

People who enjoy writing or discussing "great ideas."
Eligible men my age.
Loose as opposed to stuffy atmosphere.
A chance to get to know people over a period of time.
A chance to make new contacts through the people I
    meet here.

She then looked at her list of options, which included a local writing class, a class in contemporary literature, a series of lectures by prominent authors, a week-long writer's workshop in New England, an opportunity to work in a bookstore part-time, being part of a writers' association, and a chance to be involved in a public access TV "book show." Because she wanted to make local contacts, she ruled out the out-of-town workshop right away. She thought working at the bookstore on Saturdays might be fun, but after visiting the bookstore personally and casually talking with a friendly woman who worked there, she concluded that there really wasn't any way of determining who would be walking in the door or whether she'd ever see them again. She also didn't want work to interfere with her socializing. That still left her with several options: the two classes, the lecture series at the library, the one at a nearby city, the professional writers' group, and the TV show. Before she checked any of these out in person, she decided to do some investigating over the phone. Her conversation with the professor who taught the contemporary literature class told her all she needed to know about that option. The class was entirely lecture, so there would be little room for discussion. The professor's overly formal attitude was another option-breaker for her. She found out from the creative writing professor that his class would be primarily a discussion of the works that were brought to class by the students. He seemed enthusiastic, friendly, and perceptive over the phone. He told her she could come to one class to see if it was what she wanted. Jane decided that one was well worth checking out in person.

After talking to the librarian further, she ruled out the library lecture series because there were few, if any, eligible men there. She made it a point to check out the lecture series in the nearby city, but since the next lecture was two months away, she put it on her calendar and left it at that. Jane also called the writers' association, and the woman she spoke with told her that she had to be a published writer to join. However, the organization held workshops for aspiring writers several times a year, and one was coming up in six weeks. "What kinds of people show up at these workshops?" Jane asked the woman.

"Well, besides authors and agents, we usually get sixty to one hundred amateur and professional writers looking for tips and encouragement. And the lunch breaks and smaller discussion groups give you a chance to meet people," she said, anticipating Jane's next question. Jane thanked the woman, and put the workshop on her possible Doers list.

Meanwhile, she had begun investigating the cable TV op-

tion. She asked for the names of some of the other people involved
in that and other shows, and she called a few of these people. She enjoyed her conversations with the four people she spoke with, and
had enough in common with a woman who also had a show to
make an appointment to have lunch together. Two of the people volunteered that their involvement in their shows had enabled them to
meet people in their areas of interest, and had given them some visi-
bility in the community. On the basis of those conversations, she decided the TV show option was worth exploring further.

Jane now had three good options, but why stop there?
Even after beginning the creative writing class, signing up for the
weekend workshop, and planning her TV show, she continued to
generate ideas. On a whim, she and a friend she met at her creative
writing class decided to use the personals column to advertise for
"men and women, 25-45, who love discussing books and ideas,
who are playful and nonpretentious, for an elegant dinner followed
by stimulating conversation in our modest *salon*." Two weeks later,
Jane had received nearly two dozen replies. "Most of these letters
seem interesting," she told us. "I may have to have two events to accommodate all of these people. I never thought I was all that outgoing. In fact, I tend to be shy. But all of a sudden, I'm in the middle of
this great literary circle. There may not be many literati around this
area, but I think I've located most of them!"

KEY 16

" Singles' organizations, dating services, and personals ads might work for you—if you use them to expand your social activities network. "

With more Americans living single than ever before, a
multitude of organizations, services, options, and techniques have
sprung up to cater to single people who want to meet other singles.
The matchmakers of our grandparents' era have been replaced by
computerized dating services, singles' organizations, video dating
services, personals ads, and so on. Contrary to the popular miscon-

ception, these services are not necessarily for those who cannot meet people in the natural course of life, but for people who are too busy, or who simply don't want to put up with the time and energy-consuming hassle of qualifying new people. Dating services, singles' organizations, and personals ads are appealing because they promise a pool of already-qualified candidates. Used in this way, they can be very effective.

The pitfall of all these methods is that people often approach them with extremely high expectations, and are disappointed if they don't meet their life partner. If you do intend to join an organization, use a dating service, or place a personals ad, use the same criteria you would in qualifying any potential people-meeting arena: Is it likely to be fun? Will I be doing what I love to do? Will I be likely to meet the people I want to meet? Can I be myself in that situation? Use it as an opportunity to expand your social activities network—remember that this is your people-meeting lifeline. Don't let the focus on meeting your "one and only" get in the way of making valuable friends. Remember too, that these friends can often introduce you to new social activities networks.

While we neither encourage nor discourage your exploring these formal ways of meeting people, we do suggest you see these as just one aspect of your people-meeting plan rather than as a cure-all that will magically take care of all your needs. We also encourage you to investigate these options fully before making any commitments. The following are some criteria for checking out singles' organizations, dating services, and personals ads to help you determine whether they are for you, and if they are, how you can best use them.

DATING SERVICES

Dating services are designed for busy people and those new in the area who want to meet each other through a formal third party. This modern-day descendant of the traditional matchmaker can match people based on interests or other criteria through computer, video, personal introduction, and so on. Some services draw on a general pool of people, while others market to specific groups: for example, Jewish singles, young professionals, older people, overweight people, and the handicapped. The criteria for matching may vary from organization to organization, but generally they use written application forms designed to elicit likes and dislikes, as well as standardized personality tests and personal interviews. Usually these services contract to match you with a certain number of people over a period of time.

According to an article by Jan Broughton in *Metropolitan Detroit*, dating services must "do battle" with the stereotyped image of their clients as "desperate and dateless." Actually, their clients tend to come from all walks of life, from blue collar to professional, but with one thing in common—they want to cut through the hassle of finding someone who will be compatible in the long run. Through the battery of personality and attitude tests, dating service proponents believe they will be able to find candidates for long-term compatibility.

"When two people begin dating," Broughton quotes Joe Carruthers, marketing director for a Detroit-area dating service, "there are whole sets of difficult traits that almost any given person is going to hold back, consciously or otherwise. But when the so-called honeymoon is over, both people begin to act a little more like their normal selves. And that's when so many relationships fail—the real temperaments and tolerances of the two people are basically incompatible underneath the gloss of early infatuation."

Carruthers cautions his clients against having unrealistic hopes. "We don't promise marriage," he says, "or even necessarily the greatest romance of their lives. What we offer our clients is access to a person who has the traits and attitudes of someone with whom they'll get along very well."

The best of these services also hire investigators to screen applicants for such skeletons as criminal records and false statements, particularly about marital status. While these services can match you with others who have a similar social agenda and love-to-dos, and do away with some initial contact barriers, there are some disadvantages, mainly the cost. Dating services tend to run $1,000 and up for a five-year contract, and paying that much can create high hopes—and possible disappointment. The service may not draw on a large enough pool, particularly if you're in a certain age group. And it is too easy to focus your attention on meeting a date or mate, ignoring other equally important social agendas.

Again, meeting a mate will not solve all of your problems, nor is that one person likely to meet all of your needs. Even if you do choose to work with a dating service, your best bet is to continue to pursue the fun activities that will enable you to expand your social network on your own.

In selecting a service, as with any option, be sure to investigate fully to find out whether it's right for YOU. Ask yourself:

1. Does it seem like a fun way to meet people?
2. Will the questionnaire or interview allow me to communicate my social agenda?
3. Can I meet the kinds of people I want to meet?
4. Does the idea of selecting people on the basis of written interview or video information appeal to me?
5. Am I willing to spend the money?
6. Can I do it without expecting to meet Ms. or Mr. Right?
7. Is this a good option for me right now?

Here are some questions to ask the service:

1. What types or groups of people does your service work best for?
2. What exactly do I get for my money?
3. Is there any guarantee?
4. Are there any costs that might surface later?
5. How many people do you have from my age group, social class, with my educational level, etc.?
6. How many men? How many women?
7. Can you verify this information?
8. How many people using the service live in this area?
9. How long have you been in business?
10. Can you give me the names of some people I can call who have used this service?

Here are some questions to ask the people the service gives as references:

1. What advice would you have for someone considering using the service?
2. What are your experiences with the service, both positive and negative?
3. How long did you use the service?
4. What were the results? Were you satisfied?
5. Would you recommend the service to someone else?
6. What kind of person would this service most likely work for?

7. Do you believe you got your money's worth?

8. Do you know anyone who has used this service, but has an opinion different from yours?

The people we spoke with who owned dating services recommended that if the dating service representatives do not answer your questions to your satisfaction, call a service that will. If the service wants to protect the privacy of its clients by not giving out their names, this is understandable. However, they probably have at least a few satisfied customers they can point to who are willing to discuss the service. If they are unwilling to provide any references, consider this a red flag. You might also check the service with the local Better Business Bureau to see if any complaints have been lodged against them. If any have, it is better to know before you sign up.

SINGLES' ORGANIZATIONS

These organizations are designed to allow single people to meet over a period of time around shared activities and interests. The most successful of these organizations are focused around a specific activity—e.g., a ski club, bicycle touring society, square dancing club—or around a church group, ethnic affiliation, or life situation (Parents Without Partners, for example). Some groups, however, have little focus and can become habitual hangouts rather than places to meet new people. One of the horror stories we heard involved such a singles' organization in Florida. Liz, a forty-two-year-old manufacturer's representative, reported that since she had had difficulty meeting single men her age in Florida, she called a singles' organization she saw listed in the Yellow Pages. The man she spoke with assured her that the membership consisted of several hundred men and women, mostly active, interesting professionals. He said they had one rule she should know about: You were only allowed to check it out once. If you didn't join the first night, you could never come back as a guest. She found this a bit curious, but she decided to check it out anyway. "It was awful," she said. "There were maybe a dozen people there, and I found them passive and boring. Where were the hundreds, I wondered. The guy I spoke with on the phone turned out to be a real lounge lizard. He immediately started pressuring me to join, and I realized that there were probably hundreds who joined because they were lonely, but who stopped coming because they found something better to do—which wasn't difficult. The people who still kept coming were the residue who had nothing else going. I felt sorry for them."

Fortunately, Liz was able to uncover other singles' organizations with more of a focus around activities. She investigated a sailing club that held monthly get-togethers along with their weekly sailing classes, a "happy hour" networking group for single businesspeople, and even a singles' square dancing group. Commenting on her experiences investigating singles' organizations, Liz told us, "The advantage is that you have a ready-made group of potential friends you can get to know week after week—it's great if you enjoy the activities and the people. But be sure these are people you want to get to know before you make a commitment. I was so lonely, I almost fell for the first outfit. What a disaster that would have been!"

Other people brought up several glaring disadvantages: It might be too small or in-bred a group. Sometimes people who enjoy organizations also enjoy hierarchies and inner politics. The result can often be pecking orders and cliquishness. And if you date someone from the group, and the relationship doesn't work out, you (or the other person) might not feel like returning.

Here are some questions to ask yourself to determine if singles' organizations are the right approach for you:

1. Does joining an organization feel right to me?
2. Is there an activity involved, and is this activity something I really enjoy?
3. Have I checked it out personally, and does it feel like fun?
4. Do I have evidence that I'm likely to meet the people I want to meet here?
5. Do I feel comfortable and positive about the setting, people, activities?
6. Is there evidence that these people have other social activities networks, and am I likely to meet new friends through them?

Here are some questions to ask about the organization:

1. How many active members do you have? How many generally show up at functions?
2. What are the regularly planned activities? What is likely to happen there?

3. Who belongs to the organization? How many men? Women? Economic status? Age? Interests?

4. How much does membership cost? Are there any other expectations and duties around being a member?

5. What literature do you have available?

6. Are there some members I can talk to to get a better feel for the organization?

Here are some questions to ask the members:

1. What kinds of persons are likely to benefit most from this organization?

2. What other kinds is it not likely to work for?

3. What do you like best about the organization and its functions? What do you like least?

4. How long have you been a member?

5. What kind of person would you recommend this organization to?

6. Do you believe you are getting your money's worth? Why or why not?

7. Do you know anyone in the organization who has an opinion different from yours?

As with any option, be sure you know what you're getting into and that you have investigated the organization thoroughly before making any commitment. If your contact by telephone seems encouraging, arrange to visit for a short time. You might want to take a friend with you to get his or her perspective. If possible, don't commit the entire evening. Leave yourself room to think about it, discuss it with your friend, sleep on it. Make sure you and your friend have ample time to share impressions about the group and its members. Be aware that it might take you a few visits to get to know enough people to be able to make up your mind. Don't let yourself be pressured into joining your first night. Above all, notice if it's fun and if you enjoy the people. If so, it might be for you.

PERSONALS ADS

Over the past several years, personals ads have become a popular way of meeting people. Where once personals were the province of those interested in either kinky sex or "mail order brides," today people looking for dating partners, friends, and companions have tried placing ads. You can find these ads in newspapers, in city magazines, national magazines, and publications devoted exclusively to personals. Many people who have placed ads say it is an excellent way to break through contact barriers and be exposed to a lot of potential friends or partners with complementary social agendas. "I kept meeting creepy thirty-year-old guys looking for eighteen-year-old cuties," says Cindy, twenty-eight. "So I figured I'd advertise and drive the real prospects out of the bushes."

Personals seem to work well for people who know what they are looking for, can communicate this in words, and who can make decisions about whom they want to meet based on reading another person's ad. At the very least, personals ads offer the opportunity to define and describe exactly the kind of person you are looking for. The most distinct advantage of personals ads is that they allow you to state clearly who you are and ask directly for what you want, to state your social agenda and use the responses you get to further clarify what you are looking for. Carole told us, "In my first ad, I said among other things I was looking for a man I could 'communicate' with. I ended up with a bunch of guys who were extremely analytical, who wanted to talk everything to death. I noticed that I had this same tendency, and I was trying to change. So for my next ad, I took out 'communicate,' and had better results."

While personals ads are far less expensive than dating services, they may also be less scientific and more risky. There's no way of knowing if your respondent is telling the truth, and even the best-written ad may not insure long-term compatibility. Like dating services, personals ads can create high hopes—and big disappointments. Hugh reports: "I decided to answer an ad. A week later, the woman called me on the phone and we had what I thought was a pretty encouraging conversation. So we arranged to meet for coffee. Again we seemed to get along, although there was no chemistry to speak of. But I figured we could be friends, and introduce each other to our own social groups. But she was cool on the idea, and I wondered whether we had 'discarded' each other too soon. I had this uncomfortable feeling, like we were both furiously sorting through sale items during a 'blue light special.' "

Later on, Hugh tried placing his own ad and saw it from the other side. "At first, I was pleased because I got over twenty-five responses, but then I had to take the time to sort through and answer them. I wondered if I should answer them all, even the ones I had no interest in. Then I had to write or call the ones I did like and talk on the phone. I'd really looked forward to this phase, but I had a hard time talking to a faceless voice. It was weird. Here I was, getting to know someone I couldn't even see. Then came the meetings, and I really understood what that woman I met was going through. You meet seven or eight people, you sort of like them, but there's not the spark, and you wonder, can something develop? Is it worth pursuing? Or should you just move on to the next 'item'? I'm glad I placed the ad—I did end up with a woman I went out with a few times—but it felt like they should be called 'impersonals ads.' "

Here are some questions to ask yourself to determine if personals ads might work for you:

1. When I read personals ads, am I curious about some of the ads I see and eager to meet the people?
2. Do I have a well-formed social agenda, and can I express this in words?
3. Do I feel I can get to know people enough to prequalify them from the ads they write?
4. Do I look forward to meeting people this way? Or am I likely to feel overwhelmed or threatened by meeting so many new people in a short amount of time?
5. Will it enable me to meet the people I want to meet?
6. Does it seem like fun?
7. Will I be able to do what I love to do?
8. Can I use personals ads to expand my social activities network?

If you know anyone who has placed a personals ad, you might want to ask:

1. Why did you decide to try personals ads?
2. What were you looking for?
3. What were the results? Who responded? Were you satisfied with the people you met? How closely did the people who responded match the person you advertised for?
4. Can you offer any advice as to how to write an ad?
5. Would you do an ad again? What would you say are the advantages and disadvantages?
6. What people do you think these ads might work for? What people might they not work for?

As we said earlier, personals ads can be disappointing if you expect to find "the perfect mate." Said Linda, a thirty-year-old single parent, "I met a number of interesting men who seemed to fit my criteria, but nobody I felt that special chemistry with. I was a little discouraged until I realized that the purpose of the ad was simply to narrow the field—there was no guarantee of chemistry." As long as you approach personals ads as a way of qualifying people and not as a guarantee of finding your one and only, you stand a chance of having fun, making some new friends, and tapping into new social activities networks.

Jean reports that she answered a personals ad, met the man and didn't feel any particular romantic attraction between them. But fortunately, it didn't end there. When she told the man what she was interested in, he suggested she attend a workshop. She did, and at the workshop made a number of new friends and met someone she went out with for several months. More and more, people have begun to use personals as a way of networking—for example, the five women who advertise every month for five men to share dinner with them. This is far less threatening than a one-on-one date, and the pairing—if there is to be any—is left to the time of the meeting. Other people have advertised for people to play party games with, musicians, people for dance parties, picnics around a political or social issue, workshops, etc. If you do feel personals ads are for you, use them as a way of finding new networks of friends and fun activities—as well as in your search for a mate.

Also, take a look at *Getting Personal: Finding That Special Someone Through the Personals Ads* by Elizabeth Tener (Bantam Books, 1985) for specific tips on designing ads. Writing in *New Woman* (June, 1985) Tener suggests:

1. That you go for "quality, not quantity." In other words, make your ad specific enough to attract people you want and discourage those you don't. That way, your ad does more of the selecting work, you do less.

2. That you use common sense in protecting yourself from unwanted attention and uncomfortable situations. Use a post office box, and don't reveal your last name or phone number in the ad. When responding to an ad, you might want to give a phone number, but no last name or address. If at all possible, meet on neutral ground to make it easier for you to leave gracefully and avoid pressure.

3. That you be truthful about age ("Like it or not," she says, "it does make a difference whether a person is thirty or fifty."),

marital status, and any other factor that might be a source of surprise. Are you overweight? Refer to it positively as "teddy bear-like," or "round and cuddly." If race, religion, or nationality makes a difference, be sure to mention that.

4. That you specifically mention your positive qualities, interests, significant achievements, and anything else you feel you have to offer. The more specific, the better. "I like Bogart movies" is better than "I like movies." If you like all movies indiscriminately, say that too!

5. That you clearly state what you are REALLY looking for. Tener reports, "I would have been very happy to answer an ad from an attractive, successful, professional male, forty, divorced, who was looking for a 'vivacious, well-educated lady with interest in travel.' But for 'biking and canoeing partner'? Is this truly all he wants?"

6. That you approach the process of meeting people through personals as you would a game—you want to achieve a result, and have fun at the same time. If you approach it with unrealistic fantasies, she says, "you will unconsciously drive people away. For best results, lighten up."

And we would reiterate two other tips:

That you experiment with and modify your ad, and use it as a way to fine tune your social agenda.

That you consider an ad another tool you can use to expand your social activities networks, and that it become something you use ALONG WITH rather than INSTEAD OF you other people-meeting activities.

KEY 17

"Grow your own fun and design your own ideal people-meeting situation."

There's still another alternative to the organized activities and more formal ways of meeting that we've mentioned so far. We call it "growing your own fun," and it's ideal if you (or you and your friends) are looking for ways to apply creativity and organizing skill to your social life. Perhaps you've been unable to find your ideal people-meeting activity, or perhaps you want to add your own personal flavor. Here are some examples of how people created good times with their friends and met new people by designing an event or activity around what they love to do.

YOUR FRIENDS, MY FRIENDS, OUR FRIENDS MYSTERY DINNER   Linda, who loves fine dining, was looking for a way to enjoy good food, good conversation, new people—and a bit of adventure. So she and her new friend Jim came up with the "mystery dinner." They each contacted four of their friends who they thought would be amenable to good food and adventure. "A group of us are going to a restaurant in a nearby city," Jim and Linda told them. "The mystery is, no one but the two of us know which restaurant. Your job is to come prepared for superb food and great conversation. And you must each bring a friend we don't know." On the appointed evening, eighteen adventurous diners piled into four cars (another rule was that you couldn't ride with people you knew) and ended up at an Indian restaurant an hour away, where they had a small room and a large table to themselves.

The first mystery dinner was a resounding success. "We just sat around and talked for hours," Linda told us. "And everyone loved the food, thank goodness. Finally, it got to be time for the restaurant to close. No problem. Jim invited us all back to his house, where we continued the conversations." Another person volunteered to organize the next mystery dinner, and a new tradition was born. "We've had five or six of them," Linda reports, "and each has been special in its own way. Sometimes there are ten people, once we had almost thirty. I've made several new friends this way, and I look forward to making more."

THE BUTT KICKERS' BALL   Steve says: "I enjoy dancing, but hate bars. I had gone to one smoky bar too many when I hit upon the idea—why not a smokeless dance?" But Steve didn't have the time or the inclination to organize the event, so he did the next best thing—he found someone who would. "I called the Lung Association and suggested they use the dance as a fund-raiser. They responded enthusiastically, and the event happened without my lifting a finger." The first "Butt Kickers' Ball" attracted nearly one hundred people, and Steve made several contacts there. "It's great for someone like me who is allergic to smoke to have a pool of people to draw on who are nonsmokers. One of the women I met invited me to a nonsmokers' rights group meeting, and she said that group would help plan the next dance. The big lesson for me was, even if YOU don't want to take full responsibility for an event, you might be able to find someone who will."

COMEDY POTLUCK   Janet and several of her friends had so much fun at a comedy club that they decided to have a "comedy potluck." She invited some new friends she met at the comedy club, and some old friends, and told everyone to bring new people—and their favorite comedy records. "I specifically wanted this to be a meeting-people event," she said. "I had read a lot about how laughter breaks down barriers between people. It certainly did at the comedy club. So I decided to try it out. Everyone had such a great time, that we decided to plan the next one then and there. The second time around, people had to bring a 'real' dish and also a gag one. The one that gagged me the most was called 'maggies'—hors d'oeuvres consisting of sliced Twinkies with a tassel toothpick and pimento olive." Through these events, Janet met several new friends. "There was this one guy," she says, "that I knew from before, but not well. He really has gone into these comedy potlucks whole hog, and we've become quite close."

HEARTS AND SOULS   In one of our workshops, we helped Ruth come up with a way of combining one of her passions—playing cards—with meeting people. "I love to play 'hearts'," she told us, "but I'm not sure how to do this and meet new people." The group began brainstorming, and within ten minutes we had over a dozen ideas, including advertising an event at the local supermarket, apartment clubhouse, or work bulletin board. It was also suggested that each of her three friends bring two other guests, that they hold the event outside in the park to attract onlookers, that they work with the local Heart Association to do a "Tournament of Hearts." In the end, Ruth decided on an unadvertised party ("I don't want a large crowd, and I don't want people that no one knows") to be called "Hearts and Souls." She and a friend printed colorful, humorous invitations promising "a hearty evening of cards and dance music." At this writing, the event had not yet taken place, but Ruth told us, "If this party is half as much fun as the preparation has been, I'll be more than satisfied."

THE BARK-MITZVAH   Hank is a fun-loving character who is never at a loss for reasons to celebrate. So when his dog, Clyde, turned thirteen last year, Hank—who is Jewish—decided

that Clyde should have a bar mitzvah. Actually, it was merely an excuse for an outdoor party and picnic, but Hank sent all his friends
invitations, and encouraged them to bring friends. There was a bit
of a "bark-mitzvah" ceremony, but mainly the afternoon involved
fun in the park. Says Hank, "I find that when get-togethers have a
playful theme, it adds to the playful spirit, and makes it easier for
people to connect. I noticed that at least two of my friends met people they seemed interested in, and that's one of the purposes of the
event. That and to have fun."

    We hope these brief examples stimulated you to come up
with your own "fun-raising" events. If you have the seed of an idea
for a people-meeting event, sit down with a friend or two and brainstorm on the idea. The great thing about the brainstorm technique
is that it allows you to generate a lot of ideas without judging them.
In fact, the more outlandish the ideas, the better. After the idea-
generating phase, you can discuss, narrow, and develop the best
ideas. If you come up with what you think is a good idea, but either
don't know how to do it or are unwilling to spend the time, do what
Steve did—give the idea to someone or some organization who will
run with it. In our town, there are now hundreds of softball teams
playing in organized leagues each summer. Not many people know
that the entire softball network is traceable to one man who wanted
to play softball on a team—and who ended up organizing an entire
league! If you do choose to create a party or event, be sure YOU
have fun doing it and that you give yourself the opportunity to meet
people. On one hand, if you are the organizer of the event, meeting
people will be easier because everyone will know who you are. On
the other hand, it's easy to fall into the trap of doing too much work.
So whatever you do, be sure you have a lot of people to help you.

    Now that you have had a chance to look at how and
where you might find options, and how to narrow these down, it's
time to get moving. In the next chapter you'll learn how to create
your very own action plan—a plan that will enable you to meet the
people you want to meet.

Chapter 8

"Meeting people: your action plan"

Your objective in designing and using this action plan is to identify and select at least three qualified options for at least three of the activities you love to do. As long as you always have at least three choices—and are generating more—you will be able to select the best ones rather than settle for whatever gets tossed your way. Keep in mind that it's called an "action plan" because it demands that you act. No matter how interesting and valuable these ideas might seem, they are of absolutely no value if you don't apply them in your life.

If the idea of an action plan seems too systematic, consider this: "Peopling" your life is an extremely important project, at least as important as planning your career. Therefore, there's no reason not to be as systematic as possible in determining WHERE you go to meet the people you want to meet. Nowhere in this book do we guarantee that chemistry will happen. As far as we know, there is no way to make the right person or persons come along. But by being systematic about where you go to meet people, you can certainly increase your chances.

As suggested in the previous chapters, the process of choosing the best options includes four steps: 1) Clearly stating what you are looking for; 2) Generating options; 3) Narrowing the options; 4) Qualifying and selecting the ones you wish to pursue further.

1. CLEARLY STATE WHAT YOU ARE LOOKING FOR. Begin with the social agenda you developed in Chapter Four. In your notebook, write the social agenda at the top of the page. Is there anything you want to add to it? Any other modifications? Does it express clearly what you are looking for? Next list your criteria in order of importance: Can I do what I love there? Is it likely to be fun? Am I likely to meet the people I want to meet there? Does it appeal to me? Does it match my personality, style, likes, dislikes? Whenever you are looking for options or trying to choose from among the options you have uncovered, have this page handy to determine how each choice measures up to your agenda.

2. GATHERING OPTIONS. The purpose of this step is to seek out and identify possible options that match your social agenda. This is the "ruling in" phase where you try to find the widest range of possibilities. The more choices you have at this stage, the more choices you are likely to end up with.

- Begin with your friends and acquaintances. Make a list of all the people you know, particularly those you like. Include their addresses and phone numbers. This is your first resource list. As you look through the list, notice which people might be the easiest to call, and which might share some of your interests. Make an agreement with yourself to contact at least five of these people over the course of the week.

- As you contact friends and acquaintances, keep in mind the guidelines for gaining permission, establishing rapport, and asking for information we discussed earlier. Be sure you get them to describe possible situations and events in detail. Also, ask them if they know other people who might share your interests. As you talk with them, remember to match the options they are describing to your criteria.

- If you don't have an extensive social network, or if you wish to meet people around a specific activity, you can gather options through the Yellow Pages, classified and display advertising, bulletin boards, community calendars, and the library. You might want to take a jaunt through the Yellow Pages or *Encyclopedia of Associations* some afternoon just to stimulate your imagination. Here too, you want to keep coming back to your social agenda and criteria.

- If you are considering singles' organizations, dating services, or personals ads, go to the Yellow Pages and also consult with friends as to all the possible organizations, dating services, and publications you can use.

- And if you are considering designing your own people-meeting event, be sure you enlist your friends to help you with brainstorming and making the event a reality.

3. NARROWING YOUR OPTIONS.   Once you are satisfied that you have plenty of options to choose from, your research will take the focus of finding out as much as you need to about each option. Some you will be able to rule out quickly, others will seem like possibilities. The more carefully you do this research, the more likely you are to select options that are suitable.

- Begin by sorting your master list of places and activities into high-priority, medium-priority, and low-priority options. The high-priority options are those you strongly suspect will match your social agenda and criteria. The medium-priority options are those you really need more information about. And the low-priority items are the ones that seem like they only remotely match your criteria. Investigate the high-priority options first.

- As much as possible, get information about options from people you know. Not only are they more likely to share your perspective, but they are also likely to answer your questions frankly. Refer to the qualifying questions we mentioned in Chapter Six.

- When you talk with strangers or representatives of a group or organization, listen carefully and make sure all of your questions are answered clearly. You should have a vivid picture of each place and activity, and should be able to imagine what it might feel like to be there.

● Under each option you are considering, list both the positive and negative aspects. Refer to your criteria here.

4. SELECTING YOUR OPTIONS. Now you are ready to choose the places and activities that are most likely to match what you are looking for. Presumably at this stage you will have an abundance of good choices to choose from.

● For each activity you wish to pursue, select the three options that have the most positive and least negative aspects. Use your own criteria, and be sure that you keep in mind which of these criteria are most important to you. Although an option may have only one drawback, the drawback may be severe enough to rule it out. Likewise, it may have one overriding advantage that outweighs all the negatives.

● Make plans to personally investigate each of these options. Go with a friend if you like, but go! If it's the right place, why put off having fun? And if it isn't, it's best to get clear about that, too, so that you can move on to the next option.

● Keep in mind that you have not limited yourself in any way by selecting the options you have chosen, nor have you made any commitment by deciding to check the option out. As you prepare to visit the place, group, or situation personally, think of yourself as an investigator. And remember that anything you find out will be useful information that will help you in the future.

TIPS FOR GENERATING AND CHOOSING OPTIONS

1. Begin immediately to generate and choose options. Do something every day.

2. Make a commitment to yourself to get the results you want. Remember, the people you meet will profoundly influence your life. Here's your chance to help decide just what that influence will be.

3. **Give yourself weekly and daily objectives to accomplish.** Be sure these objectives are clear and do-able. Write them down and review them at the end of each week. Did you accomplish what you set out to do? Did you challenge yourself too much? Too little?

4. **Do this with a friend.** Compare notes and give each other support and encouragement.

5. **Remind yourself that you can enjoy the process as well as the results.** If you get stuck or you feel the process isn't working for you, take a break; do something that makes you feel better.

6. **Modify this information to fit YOUR OWN style.** If planning and research isn't your thing, do whatever it takes to turn it into fun.

7. **Keep the goal in mind at all times.** Don't get so caught up in making lists and organizing information that you forget the purpose—to meet people and have fun.

8. **Keep a meeting-people notebook.** As we suggested earlier, writing down goals and action plans helps to make your goals and plans more real. You might want to carry your daily and weekly objectives on three-by-five file cards so that you can refer to them over the course of the day.

9. **Decide how much time you will spend each week.** Schedule time on your weekly calendar, and make it one of your top priorities. Make a commitment to follow through each week. We found that the people who consistently followed through consistently got results.

10. **Do whatever it takes to motivate yourself.** Give yourself credit for every step you take.

Chapter 9

"Overcoming 'stoppers': getting out of the funk and into the fun"

One thing we noticed time and time again while conducting our interviews for this book—people who enjoy meeting people and are successful at it rehearse their success beforehand and immerse themselves in thoughts of what a great time they are going to have when they get there. At the same time they are rehearsing having a great time, they are careful not to overanticipate the people they are going to meet. They know they have far more influence over what kind of time they have than whether they will meet a special person. By preparing to enjoy themselves, they are creating the right mood and environment for meeting someone.

The fact is, having an experience and thinking about that experience are pretty much the same. Right now, imagine yourself about to eat a juicy hamburger or a hot fudge sundae. If you are at all hungry, you will find yourself salivating at just the thought of eating. The central nervous system really can't tell the difference between a dish of ice cream in front of us and one in our minds. Now imagine eating a lemon. Your mouth is probably already puckering at the thought of that tart juice. Do you anticipate lemons when it comes to meeting people?

KEY 18

"What you believe about what will happen can strongly influence what does happen."

There is a now-classic story of an experiment done in an elementary school. Before the school year began, teachers were informed that a test given to their students revealed that certain students could be expected to make great gains that year. Although no test was actually given, the experimenters told the teachers which students to expect "great things" from, then sat back to await the results. Not surprisingly, the students whose success was predicted by the mythical test did score better grades than other students of equal ability. Not only that, but they actually DID make measurable gains that year on standardized tests! Of course, beliefs can work the other way as well. Those equally gifted students who were not expected to improve, didn't. Because the teachers' basic beliefs about these "gifted" students changed, their behavior changed as well. They treated these kids differently.

When we believe certain things about ourselves or other people, our behavior will reflect those beliefs. There is nothing magical about the relationship between beliefs and behavior. Alex anticipates future events by reliving times he has been turned down. He is so prepared to be turned down that he asks women to dance by saying, "You wouldn't want to dance with me, would you?" And they usually don't.

Although she is a thirty-year-old woman, Mary still feels like an awkward adolescent. Many times she has had the opportunity to talk to men, but instead talked herself out of it because of a belief that they would not be interested. Attitudes are beliefs about experience. We are often unaware of our attitudes and how they shape our feelings, expectations, and what we get out of life. It's a good bet that if you're dissatisfied with the results you are getting, the seeds of this dissatisfaction can be found in your attitudes about what can and will happen.

Your attitudes can work for you or against you. One way to find out what you believe is to listen to what you say, both out loud and to yourself. Ask a close friend to listen to your conversation over the course of an evening and give you feedback as to the language you are using. Or take fifteen minutes or so to listen to your own thoughts. Are you constantly criticizing yourself and judging others? Are you patting yourself on the back? Do you look forward to social situations, events, new people? Do you look at strangers as people to be very wary of, or as "unmet friends"? Do you spend mental energy anticipating problems that haven't come up yet? Do you anticipate fun times? You might be surprised at what you find out. Be on the lookout for negative attitudes like the ones listed below. These are robbing you of good times and getting in the way of meeting the people you want to meet.

MENU OF NEGATIVE ATTITUDES

I feel uncomfortable with new people and situations.

I am not attractive.

I never know what to say; I feel as if I'll be boring people.

I feel awkward in social situations.

All the good men/women are taken.

I don't really know how to start conversations with others.

If I'm attracted to someone, he's probably uninterested or unavailable.

I'll probably never get what I want.

Most people are selfish (or callous, or not interested in me).

Women should not approach men/ men should not let themselves be approached by women.

I feel uncomfortable saying "No."

If I let someone get close, she'll only leave me or disappoint me.

I don't have the time to go out and meet people.

There's no place out there where I can be comfortable and meet the kinds of people I want to meet.

Men are only interested in one thing/ women are just out to trap you.

It is normal to have these kinds of feelings at some time in your life. It's what you do with them and the extent to which they limit your enjoyment of living that's important. Once you've decided that you would like to change an attitude or feeling, the first step is to understand how having that attitude or feeling has helped you in the past—and might even be helpful in the future. For example, the attitude "New people and situations make me uncomfortable" reflects the legitimate concern that there are people and situations out there in the world that might be harmful to you. If you use this feeling or attitude as a "watchdog" to alert you to potentially unpleasant experiences, it can be a useful attitude to have. If, however, this belief keeps you from meeting ANY new people or checking out ANY new situations, the belief is no longer working for you—you are its slave.

Notice which of the above attitudes get in the way of your meeting people. Make a list of these, and add any others that have stopped you in the past. Ask yourself the following questions: What does having this attitude or belief do for me? What would eliminating or changing it do for me? Might there be a more positive way to get the same benefit? How can I turn around this unwanted attitude? Says Wendy, "I thought I was a poor conversationalist, that I never had anything interesting to say." When she looked at this attitude more carefully, she realized she used the attitude to keep from reaching out towards people she was interested in meeting. By waiting for them to approach her first, Wendy protected herself. That way, she could be sure they were interested. Wendy decided she could protect herself from embarrassment or disappointment by taking small steps in the direction of the people she wanted to meet, and using shared activities and interests as a bridge to conversation.

Not long after she made that decision, Wendy was on a Sunday morning ride with a local bike club. When they stopped for breakfast, she noticed one of the men she'd been wanting to meet standing a few feet away from her. "As I thought about approaching him," she says, "I had this thought running through my head, 'but what am I going to say?' Then I remembered to smile and relax, and I figured I had nothing to lose. As I walked by him, I smiled and said, 'hi,' and the conversation started just like that. We started out talking about our biking experiences, but very quickly we were sharing other things about ourselves. When he mentioned that his field was molecular biology, instead of feeling intimidated because I didn't know anything about the subject, I just said, 'Gee, I don't know much about that field. What do you do?' It was such a relief to be able to confess to being ignorant, and I really enjoyed his explanation. When the conversation turned to what I love to do, I felt he was really listening. Later, he actually told me what a great conversationalist I was. Now, whenever I felt apprehensive about being able to keep up a conversation, I just play back that incident as a reminder that I don't have to worry about being interesting."

Keep in mind that "turning around" unwanted attitudes does not necessarily mean discarding them completely; instead, it means making sure they work for you, and giving yourself other choices as well. Cynthia, who recently moved to the Midwest from New York City, used to feel quite guarded around new people. "It was hard for me to return smiles and look at people directly," she says. "I felt like there was something wrong with me until I realized that in New York that's just not done. As a lifetime New Yorker, I had adopted that guarded attitude. So I'm consciously trying to be more open. Even if I can't be as relaxed as I'd like, I can still tell people, 'you know, I'm just not used to people being so open, so I hope you'll excuse my awkwardness.' I find that in just mentioning the differences in cultures, I feel more comfortable with new people and they're relieved to find it isn't anything they've done." Cynthia has learned that even an undesired attitude can be turned into an asset—and a bridge to others.

KEY 19

"When you feel good about yourself, it's easy to attract others."

The people who are most successful at meeting other people are those who genuinely feel good about themselves, the situation, and others—and project that good feeling. All of us from time to time will feel bad, unsociable, noncommunicative. Changes in mood are normal. But habitually feeling bad can be a damaging habit. What you feel inside can often be read on your face and in your behavior, and send others the message: "Keep away." Fortunately, you have far more control over your moods than you might suspect. One simple way of turning around the habit of feeling bad is to replace your negative memories with brand new positive experiences, experiences you get from reaching out to others and enjoying yourself.

Jack attended one of our seminars, and shared a realization he had about his mother. "She would always bemoan the fact that no one ever came to visit us," Jack said. "But the fact is, she never invited anyone!" It's easy to sit back and wait for good things to happen to you. Perhaps at some time in your life, potential friends simply appeared. Neighborhoods, schools, even work can provide a natural network of friends. However, life situations change. What might have been easy in high school is no longer easy when you live in a huge apartment complex and do most of your work alone or with just a few people. In that situation, it is easy to let time go by without making overtures to others—and then conclude that no one really wants to spend time with you anyway.

Charles, another seminar participant, shared this about himself: "For a long time now, I've been feeling apart from others. And it seems that the more isolated I feel, the less I want to be with others. So it's a vicious circle. I had to force myself to come to this workshop. But since I felt I had hit rock bottom, I didn't feel I had much to lose. The funny thing is, as soon as I began participating and becoming a part of things, I began to feel more connected." As simplistic as it may sound, the best cure for feeling isolated is actively reaching out for social contact!

Says Jennifer, "I was really depressed, introverted, lacking motivation. I dwelled on my loneliness and expected people to come to me. Finally, it got to the point where I was feeling so low, it was either up or out. First, I made the decision that I was going to change my situation. As soon as I started to feel down, I would reach out for others instead of expecting them to reach out for me. Or I would do something for someone. That, I found, would automatically make me feel better. I also decided that meeting people could be fun. I began to take risks and enjoyed interacting with people just in the moment." Sometimes simply deciding—as Jennifer did—is enough to motivate yourself. But sometimes, it is necessary to speak with a counselor, therapist, clergyman, or someone else whose job it is to help people with personal problems. Just as we don't hesitate to consult a physician if we are having physical symptoms, it makes just as much sense to consult an expert if emotional difficulties are getting in the way of enjoying life.

Another way to turn around negative feelings and attitudes is to build a firm foundation for feeling good within yourself. "The only time I felt stuck about meeting people was right after my divorce, when I felt low about myself," says Lindsey. "But then, I began to do things for ME, like jogging and exercising. I bought a whole new set of clothes to go with my new body. I changed my hair style, and got a new car. I began to buy the music I love and went to concerts with friends. I started attending a new church, and for the first time I began to feel an inner peace. I think all of this helped when I told my friends I was ready to meet new men. This whole process took about eighteen months, and I think it was worth it to prepare myself by liking me first. I knew I was ready when I began to like myself. And my friends told me that it showed."

Diane had a similar experience. "After I split up with the man I'd been with for three years, I didn't feel ready to be in another relationship," she says, "so I decided to immerse myself in things I never had time for when I was 'coupled.' I took up running again, and I found that I loved the solitude and the challenge. When I worked my way up to seven miles, I decided that I would train to run a marathon—twenty-six miles. It took several months of vigorous and difficult training, but I did my marathon. Of course, I've met lots of new friends through my interest in running. But more important to me right now is the change in my self-esteem. Everyone has noticed it." As Diane discovered, the best way to give yourself "an esteem bath" is to immerse yourself in activities you love.

From time to time, just about everyone feels "I'm not attractive enough." The quickest way to turn this around is to remember that it is fun and happiness that are attractive. Says Julie, "I used to feel self-conscious at big gatherings, as if I were being compared with the other women there. So I would hold back, and maybe even come off as a bit cold. I figured if I were too friendly, guys wouldn't be attracted to me. At the urging of a friend, I tried an experiment. I asked a number of men I knew and liked what traits they found attractive. I was surprised when so many of them listed friendliness. Now I feel more comfortable smiling—and more attractive."

Feeling unattractive can have at least one real benefit—it can spur you to activity that can make you more attractive. Of course, physical appearance makes a difference. To most people, being neat and well groomed is more attractive than being sloppy. The way you look is an important statement about yourself, and is often the only statement about you people get. Does your appearance invite people to move closer, or does it put people off? Remember here we are not talking about "good looks," but what we can do to improve what we have. You can do what Lindsey did and lose weight and buy new clothes and change hairstyles. More important, you can do more of the things you enjoy and get satisfaction from—as she listened to more music and attended a new church—because ultimately, attractiveness is something that radiates out from your own positive feeling about yourself.

Look again at the list of negative attitudes, and pay attention to the ones that seem familiar to you. Are there any of these that can be changed by bringing more pleasure, contact, adventure into your life, by doing more of the things you love to do? Do you keep hearing a little voice that says, "It's not going to work, it's not going to work"? Make a pledge to yourself that you will try these new things EVEN THOUGH you feel they might not work. The fact is, they might not work. But what have you got to lose? If you're feeling lonely and isolated, what you might have to lose is loneliness and isolation. Certainly that's worth an experiment.

KEY 20

" The best way to handle fears of a 'bad scene' is to choose your situations well, and know how you intend to handle sticky situations— before you go out. "

There's an old vaudeville joke where a man goes to the doctor, flexes his arm and says, "Doctor, it hurts when I do this."

"So don't do this," is the doctor's reply. "That'll be twenty dollars, please."

Why is it that we so often repeat painful situations, even knowing they are going to cause us pain? How many times have we said to ourselves, "You know, I knew all along such-and-such was wrong, but I went ahead and did it anyway?" Marla accepted a Sunday morning breakfast date from a man she liked but barely knew. When he arrived to pick her up, he told her there had been a change of plans. Instead of having breakfast at the restaurant he had suggested, they would be visiting some friends of his in the country. "For some reason, I felt really uncomfortable with this change of plans," Marla told us, "but I just talked myself into going. I didn't want to be a stick-in-the-mud or a complainer."

All the way out to the country, Marla tried to disguise her discomfort by making small talk. When they arrived the people date brought out the drugs. It wasn't that Marla had never been around drugs before. She just didn't like them, and now her discomfort turned to a sense of danger. "I didn't know who these people were, but I was stuck there with them. Worse than that, I had to rely on my date for a ride home, and I was afraid he was too stoned to drive." Marla finally called a cab. Her confused date offered to pay for half of the cab fare, but Marla told him to forget it. "I have since learned," she says, "that it's more important for me to find out what's going on beforehand than for a guy to think of me as a good sport. And I'm a lot less reluctant to say no when I'm not satisfied with what I've heard."

One of the most common reasons for talking ourselves into less-than-perfect situations is a lack of choices. How many times have you gone to bars, parties, on blind dates, to play miniature golf, just because there was nothing else happening? How many times have you agreed to spend time with someone you didn't want to spend time with because it was something to do? Later, you came home saying, "Why did I do that? I should have known better."

Another common problem—especially among women—is the inability to say no. "A man at work sort of attached himself to me," says Julie, a teacher. "Although I didn't give him any overt signs of being interested, he kept hanging around. Finally, when he heard I was going on an outward-bound type camping trip, he asked if he could come along. I didn't really want to be with him on my vacation, but I just couldn't bring myself to say no, even though NO was screaming in my head. Of course, the vacation was a disaster. Even though he got the hint and let me alone, he didn't really fit with the group. And everyone saw him as 'Julie's friend.' The funny thing is, after all that, I'm not sure I could say no to him in the future. I'm just afraid of hurting people's feelings."

As you look back on your list of "stopper" attitudes, notice if an ability to say no to unwanted people and experiences would help you avoid certain experiences so that you don't have to avoid *all* new experiences. Martha, another woman we spoke with, revealed, "One of the reasons I don't go to parties much is because I hate to be in the position of turning guys down, even if it's a guy I'm not at all interested in. Sometimes men will ask me to dance or ask me for my phone number or even just want to have a conversation and if I'm not interested, I have a hard time getting it across. At times, I end up enduring a conversation I don't want to be in just to be polite. So I figure it's much easier to avoid those situations entirely by staying home."

Jean finds herself with a different problem. "When I say no," she says, "men don't take me seriously. They think I'm playing some kind of game with them. Or else they get visibly hurt or offended, and I feel like the bad guy. I wish I could get the point across, but more and more I find myself staying away from situations where I might encounter persistent strangers." Can you see how Martha and Jean are paying the price for their inability to gently, yet firmly, say no? One of your rights as an adult human being is your right to "No." You need never give an excuse or rationalization for turning down any experience you don't want to have. By preparing yourself for saying no beforehand, you will feel more confident and comfortable in new situations—and more likely to say yes to things you want. Here are some ways to say no with confidence and without putting the other person down.

TIPS FOR DECLINING INVITATIONS

1. **Simply smile and say, "No, thank you."** Remember, you owe another person nothing more than politeness. You are not required to give a reason unless you want to.

2. **If you are interested in the person and not the activity, say so.** Mention some things you'd rather do, and see if she's interested in them, too.

3. **If you are interested in neither the person nor the activity, but appreciate being asked, "sandwich" the no between two statements that express appreciation for the person.** This can be tricky and seem contrived if you have to grope for things to say, but if you genuinely appreciate being asked, by all means do this. An example would be, "I enjoyed talking with you this evening, but I don't really want to go downhill hot-tub hopping. Thanks for the invite, though."

4. **If the person continues to ignore all of your firm yet gentle signals, move on to another person or group.** As long as you stand there and talk with someone who's being inappropriate, he will believe he has a chance to wear down your resolve. Actions speak louder than words. At the first signs of discomfort, move away from that person as quickly as possible. Don't wait for real problems to occur; trust your early warning system.

If you tend to let your beliefs about other people stop you from going out and having fun, now is the time to take steps to choose what's right for you and stick to it. Ask questions. Find out beforehand if a person or situation is for you. If it isn't, say no. If you believe that things simply happen to you, you are a prime candidate for an unpleasant experience. Researching, choosing well, and paying attention as you go are the best ways to protect yourself from a bad time.

KEY 21

"Use the '3 for 1' rule to create three positives for every negative."

Remember that negative signals may have positive influence—they can warn you of a potentially unpleasant experience. And you can also use them as a jumping-off point toward getting more of what you DO want. Think of how much time you spend with friends complaining and bemoaning horrible encounters with insensitive people. Here's how to turn those around: for everything you decide you don't want, think of three things you do want. We call this the "3 for 1" rule. Make a picture of each of the three things you do want. When the picture is clear, step into it and notice how it feels. Then change anything that is not exactly right.

Take Joe, for example. He's noticed that he tends to get involved with "passive-aggressive" women who manipulate rather than clearly express what they want. Joe has decided that in the future he wants to avoid women with this trait. He's also decided to use the "3 for 1" rule so that he's clear about what he *is* looking for. So he identifies three positive traits that represent the opposite of passive-aggressive: "I want to meet a woman who tells me clearly what she likes and doesn't like, who has high self-esteem, and who genuinely likes men." Since these traits can mean different things for different people, Joe makes a picture so he knows what each means to him. He uses the picture to further refine what he wants.

In his mind, Joe goes back to a woman he knew who gave clear messages about her likes and dislikes. He frowns, however, because her tone of voice was harsh and resentful. So he simply changes her tone to a pleasant one; instead of feeling criticized or put down, he now feels she has simply given him information. Because he has played the scenario over in his mind's eye, he now has a picture to go with the words "tells me clearly what she likes and dislikes." He then makes another picture for "high self-esteem," and one for "genuinely likes men." And he makes whatever adjustments are necessary to create a vivid picture of what he is looking for.

Use the "3 for 1" rule anytime you discover something you don't want. To repeat, there's nothing wrong with stating what you don't want—as long as you use those negatives as an opportunity to discover three times as many things you *are* looking for. That way, you are moving toward your goal—and away from what you *don't* want.

KEY 22

"The more realistic your expectations, the less likely you are to be disappointed."

One of the most common causes of disappointment and frustration when it comes to meeting people is unrealistic expectations. There are a lot of people who deprive themselves of feeling successful by putting "success" out of reach. Take Jack for example. Recently divorced, he decided his life would be complete if only he could meet Ms. Perfect. So he went to party after party, singles' event after singles' event, but still no Ms. Perfect. Even though he was meeting women, he would measure them against his rigorous criteria and if they didn't fit, he wouldn't bother getting to know them better.

At a square dance, Jack found himself having a great time. Just to have a partner, he asked a woman to dance. "Even though she didn't seem to be my type," Jack says, "she was really friendly and seemed to have a spirit about her. We kept on talking during the break, and before the evening was over, I had accepted a dinner invitation from her." Jack ended up going out with the woman for several months, and although it didn't end in marriage, Jack feels it was one of the most valuable relationships he has ever been in. "I didn't realize how bitter and isolated I had become," he says. "Janet reintroduced me to having fun. And she appreciated the way I supported her in her career plans. I was surprised at how easily she accepted that I didn't look at her as a permanent life partner. What a pleasure to be in a relationship without a lot of jealousy and drama! It was new for me. It made me wonder how many other great friendships I had passed up just because I ruled people out too quickly."

If you've been frustrated because you haven't met the "right" person, the antidote might be to limit your expectations to simply having fun. Keep your social agenda in mind by all means, but don't let it get in the way of your good time. You'll know if people qualify for further contact by getting to know them while having fun, in the natural course of events.

As songwriter Michael Franks says, "Love is like baseball." Even the greatest batters fail to get a hit two out of every three times at bat. Instead of viewing themselves as "failures," hitters like to say that their job is to make contact and the hits will take care of themselves. This is good advice for the people-meeting game as well. Make contact with enough people and you can rest assured you will have your share of hits.

One of the unfortunate by-products of looking for the Perfect Person and having little success is the belief, "I'll NEVER find the right person" and its corollary, "I keep finding the wrong people." Such a belief can result in not bothering to go out at all ("I mean, what's the use?") or else looking so downcast that only a professional rescuer or a certified masochist would even dream of making contact. Brenda reports, "A friend suggested that I make a list of the attributes that I wanted in a man. Well, I did this, but the emptiness of not having someone like this only made me feel worse. How was I ever going to find someone like that? My friend heard me say, 'An attractive, successful man who likes himself and communicates well is hard to find' and suggested I turn the thought around to, 'It is now easy to find an attractive, successful man who likes himself and communicates well.' Even though this seemed a little ridiculous, I found myself feeling more positive and up about meeting people."

Later that week, Brenda put the positive statement on an endless loop cassette and listened to it on and off during the next two days. While listening to the tape, she realized that a part of her objected to meeting a man out of fear she would be hurt. She took care of that concern by promising herself "to pick well and protect myself." Two weeks later, she met a man at a discussion group. They went out dancing, then to dinner—and a year and a half later they were married. We hesitated to tell this story because of the "magical" ring it has to it. All the same it is true. There's no guarantee that changing your negative beliefs will automatically result in you meeting the right person. But it will be easier to get started, and with your eyes open to the positive possibilities, you will be more likely to notice the right person when he or she appears. Changing your attitudes is like chicken soup—it couldn't hurt.

TIPS FOR TURNING AROUND
UNHELPFUL ATTITUDES

1. Give yourself an "esteem bath" by listing all the things you like about yourself. This can include anything from your sense of humor to the fact that you have great knees. Then ask your friends to add to the list. Look at the list anytime you're preparing to go out and meet new people, or anytime your self-esteem needs a boost.

2. Do whatever you need to do each day to feel attractive and desirable. Carry something like a photo, an inspirational quote, a note, or other reminder with you that will stimulate you to feel good about you.

3. Pamper yourself. If you are telling yourself "downer" stuff, feeling bad in general, or seeing the world in a negative frame, give yourself a break. Take a long, hot bath or shower and sing until you are so satisfied you can hardly stand it.

4. Try this experiment for a week. If you believe it will require twelve years of therapy to really change your attitudes, pretend you are genuinely happy and enthusiastic. Notice the results.

5. Begin a self-renewal project to improve your self-image. Start an exercise routine, buy some new clothes, or pursue new activities and interests. Ask for feedback from friends, and use your renewal project to meet and make contact with new people.

6. Participate, don't vegetate. People who are physically active every day—jogging, walking, bouncing on their bouncer, playing tennis—report that activity tends to put them in a more positive mood. Put on some upbeat music and dance for a half hour. Then take a walk. We've heard lots of great stories of people changing their moods and getting moving that way. It might work for you.

7. Develop a talent. Music, photography, painting, and writing promote active self-expression. Share this talent with others.

8. Do something every day to meet people or to feel better about yourself. Remember that change occurs one day at a time, one step at a time. Make sure you give yourself credit for every step you take no matter how it turns out. Keep a journal and share your progress with a friend you trust.

9. When you think about the past, reach into the treasure chest, not the dumpster. Review your past successes in relating to people, specifically how much they enjoyed you. This can be a great confidence builder. One of the most effective ways to connect with others is by sharing stories about great times you've had. Really enjoy these past experiences—they are an invaluable resource.

10. Choose your situations wisely. Know beforehand how you will handle an unpleasant or sticky situation.

11. If you feel uncomfortable about an upcoming social event, look for the source of that discomfort. Ask yourself if the upcoming event matches both your social agenda and your idea of a good time. If it doesn't, consider doing something else.

12. Practice saying no to the people and situations you don't want. Then you can unequivocally say yes to those you do want.

13. Remember to use the "3 for 1" rule. Use what you don't want as a stepping-stone to what you do want.

14. Get out into the world of people and make contact. Even if it just involves saying hello and talking about the weather, give yourself permission to meet people your own way at your own pace. Go only as far as you are comfortable, and do only those things that bring you joy and satisfaction. Begin doing this TODAY!

15. Don't wait for others to call you first. Do active detective work to find things you love to do and people to do them with. Call and ask other people what they feel like doing, and tell them what you feel like doing. THEN DO IT!

16. Go on a mission to seek out new options. Remember Chapter Seven? Look in newspapers, at the library, and ask people you already know. Then follow up on those options.

17. Make it an adventure to try out new places and new events. When you feel fearful about making contact with new people, remember that fear is just excitement in disguise.

18. Do your homework. If you find yourself thinking that there aren't enough available people in your age group, go to the library and look at the population statistics for the nation and your local area. You might be surprised to find out just how many eligible people there are out there.

19. Do something for someone else. There are lots of people who can use help. Volunteer through some organization in the community, and use the experience to make contact with others.

20. You're not the only person who needs and wants company. Remind yourself that others want to meet you for all the reasons you want to meet them.

21. Be aware that you can have a good time with people just by having a conversation about what you really love to do.

22. Instead of trying to impress people, find out what they love to do, what they are really interested in by asking them tactful questions about themselves. If you find yourself prejudging people, let yourself be curious about them instead. You may be surprised and delighted with what you find out.

23. Notice the little things about yourself and others that you like and appreciate. If you are used to nitpicking and finding fault with yourself and others, start using the same skill to find out what's right about people.

24. Expect people to be exactly the way they are. Accept both the positive and negative traits in yourself and others as part of our uniqueness.

Remember that the easiest way to change your attitudes is through new experiences, and you can choose your new experiences. Choose wisely, and choose fun. Don't wait—get started now!

Chapter 10

"Preparing to have fun by having fun preparing"

You're more than halfway through this book, and already things are looking better. You've begun spending more time doing what you love to do, and you've started meeting new people. Last week, for example, you met a new acquaintance playing tennis, and he invited you to a Friday night get-together at his tennis club. You thought about calling him up during the week to find out more details, but somehow you never quite found the time. "That's all right," you say to yourself cheerfully as you walk out the door, "I'll be surprised."

Your enthusiasm is dampened a bit as you drive around for forty-five minutes looking for the place. Maybe I should have gotten directions, you think. Finally, you arrive and you're even more surprised than you expected. There you are in your tennis outfit—and everyone else is dressed to the teeth. Oh well, you think. This will make me more noticeable. After a few minutes, you begin to feel really uncomfortable. Painfully aware of your naked knees, you try to hide in a corner over near the bathroom. Fortunately, you spy an old acquaintance, and you spend the rest of the evening in the same corner of the clubhouse talking with this one person. When the evening is over, you realize that in your embarrassment about wearing the wrong thing, you forgot you had a social agenda. Consequently, you didn't do anything to meet anyone new. And you didn't meet anyone.

Or perhaps you're the kind of person who loves to plan and anticipate. You love good food and now you've been invited to a gourmet potluck. You decide to make the squid Florentine that wowed 'em at the company picnic last summer. You can picture the adoring smiles of the guests as they taste your culinary gem—and maybe, just maybe that one person you are looking for will be there. "Who made this extraordinary squid Florentine?" that person will ask. And you will step forward, smiling modestly, and showing lots of eyelid. It would be love at first bite.

You plunge yourself into making the dish as if it were the Perfect Person and not the food that you were concocting. You spend an hour in the fish market, choosing the squid as carefully as you would a wedding outfit. For an event like this, only the right squid will do. You spend Thursday evening painstakingly creating the dish that will change your life, all the while seeing that Perfect Person nodding in approval. It's an exhausting task and hasn't been much fun, but wait'll they see it! When you finally go to bed, it's 4:30 a.m.

Two hours later, you drag yourself out of bed to go to work. At work, you are, as your twelve-year-old would say, "a walking waste product." Somehow you make it through the day, come home and crash. A phone call awakens you. It's your friend. "Where are you? We're already into the hummingbird-liver paté and ready for the next course. If you don't hurry, you're going to miss the whole thing!" In your stupor, you forgot to set the alarm. You throw yourself together the best you can, and get there in time to get the last serving of grapefruit mousse. Your squid stands untouched on the table, and you are inconsolable. Seeing the other guests talking and having fun only makes you feel worse. You don't even look for the Perfect Person at the gathering; you feel unworthy. Sadly, you realize that you became so involved in anticipation that you forgot to handle the all-important detail of getting there on time. As carefully as you prepared the squid, you neglected to prepare yourself.

Or maybe you're the kind of person who gets really excited at the prospect of going out and meeting new people. But along with the excitement comes a twinge of anxiety. You've been invited to a film opening where there'll be lots of people who share your interest in movies, and yet you keep thinking of all the awkward moments in the past when you tried to meet people but just couldn't think of the right thing to say. Or the times when you did meet people and things didn't work out. Instead of focusing on the new movie you are about to see, your mind keeps playing the old "movies" of your less-than-perfect encounters with new people. And you notice your enthusiasm for going to this opening beginning to wane. "Maybe I'm just setting myself up for disappointment by going out," you say to yourself, and you begin to find a long list of reasons why the event won't be much fun. Suddenly, you realize you have a headache. It seems like a perfect evening to curl up with a good book or watch "Loveboat" reruns on TV.

Or maybe you are able to motivate yourself to go somewhere to meet people—such as the stress management seminar you've been looking forward to—but on the way over you find yourself reliving an argument with the person you recently broke up with. By the time you get there, you are convinced that all (or at least most) members of the opposite sex possess the same irritating traits as your "ex." As you listen to the discussion, all you seem able to focus on is what you dislike about these new people. As a result, you feel guarded all evening. You hang back from participating, and become an observer lost in the conversation inside your own head. A few times you consider talking to someone, but you think better of it. "Why bother?" you say to yourself. "There's no one here I'm interested in anyway." You return home a bit dejected, but there's a little glimmer of triumph. "At least," you say, "I didn't expect much so I wasn't too disappointed."

KEY 23

" Whether you prepare or not, you are always preparing. "

Perhaps these disappointing experiences—exaggerated as they might be—have a familiar ring. While some disappointment is inevitable in your encounters with new people, you can minimize disappointment, anxiety, and unrealistic expectations just in the way you prepare yourself. Since the best way to meet people is by having fun, when you prepare yourself for fun—and let meeting people be the natural outgrowth of having a good time—you will be more likely to have realistic expectations and present your most relaxed, likable self. If you're not satisfied with the results you are getting when it comes to meeting people, you might want to look at how you are preparing.

The first thing to understand is that whether you are aware of it or not, whether you are consciously doing so or not, you are always preparing. The person who rushes off to a get-together without getting directions or checking to see which outfit would be appropriate is preparing by not preparing. Since that person has not considered beforehand how he could pursue a social agenda, he ends up reacting to what is happening rather than making things happen. Since he has not prepared to make things happen, he is limited to only the choices that are presented. "I'll be surprised," he said as he left his house. Unfortunately, the surprise was not the kind he had in mind.

At the other extreme is the person who prepares by overpreparing and overanticipating, and as a result is almost guaranteed disappointment. The person who fixed the gourmet dish became so absorbed in that one aspect of preparing that she lost sight of everything else. After spending all her time cooking, she was too tired to enjoy herself. Had she taken the time to prepare her own mood by anticipating the fun of the event instead of her imagined meeting with Mr. Perfect, she might have been able to put things in perspective. She might have decided to prepare another dish instead or find a short-cut so that she could have gone to bed earlier and awakened more rested.

Instead of fully enjoying the process of cooking, she turned it into a difficult chore with a payoff down the line. What carried her through her culinary heroics was the unrealistic vision of who might be at the dinner and how he might react. A little fantasy can give incentive and spark your enthusiasm about going out; but if having the fantasy come true in definite, predefined terms becomes the only criterion for having a good time, your odds of having a good time are not very good. A woman in one of our seminars told the group that only once in her life did she have success meeting someone. As the discussion developed, it became apparent that HER definition of success meant the meeting led to marriage! When you consider that even the most oft-married among us get married three to four times at the most, that's an awful lot of disappointment. If you go to a social event once a week for twenty years and meet three marriage partners, you will be disappointed 99.7 percent of the time!

The biggest problem faced by the overpreparers and overanticipators is that they're so focused on the outcome while preparing that they forget to have fun, even if it's an activity—like cooking—that they love to do. Once at the event, they are so busy looking for Ms. or Mr. Perfect that they fail to appreciate the people they do meet. They spend so much time looking forward to some future situation that they forget to simply relax and have fun in the present. Consequently, they miss out on a great opportunity to enjoy themselves, enjoy the present situation, and enjoy others.

The people who prepare by remembering past disappointments may talk themselves out of going at all, or their negative anticipation of the future based on negative memories of the past can lead to a self-fulfilling prophecy. While anyone can be stymied by memories of negative experiences from time to time, the negative anticipator tends to get caught in an endless loop. For that person, there are few new experiences—just replays of old negative ones. Even with a conscious, positive intention to have a good time, when past experiences cause you to take a dim view of the future, you aren't likely to enjoy yourself. As you'll see later in the chapter, the antidote for this Negative Preparation Syndrome is to stop worrying about the outcome and immerse yourself in thinking about how much fun you're going to have. You'll still be "rehearsing," but the rehearsal will be based on a desired future, not a disappointing past.

By now, you're probably aware of how YOU prepare to go out and meet people. You may tend to just "show up" without consciously preparing, you might have a tendency to overanticipate or overprepare, or you might prepare by referring to past experiences. Whichever is your way, in this chapter you will learn to take the best of what you are already doing, and use past experience, present preparation, and positive anticipation to constructively influence your future good times. You will also learn how to have a great time preparing, so no matter what the outcome, the time you spend preparing will be revitalizing rather than exhausting. And because you are going out at your best—in a positive mood, radiating enjoyment of self and enjoyment of others, you will be much more likely to meet the people YOU want to meet.

KEY 24

"Having your own positive preparation plan is like starting the party early."

If you think back on the most enjoyable times in your life, you will remember them with a pleasant afterglow. You can think of the positive preparation routine you will now develop as a "pre-glow" that will allow you to begin enjoying the event before it begins. You can create this pre-glow by feeling good in the present and combining what has worked in the past with what could work in the future. The following exercise is designed to get you in touch with what YOU use to prepare your "fun" self to go out and have a great time.

Begin by sitting in a comfortable chair where you will be undisturbed for a few minutes. When you are comfortable and relaxed, close your eyes, and in your mind's eye scan your memory for times when you really enjoyed yourself meeting new people. Run through the experience, start to finish, as if you were watching a movie. Do this slowly, so as to notice every detail. Play the movie again, if necessary, and see if you can find details you missed the first time around. Notice your surroundings, the other people, anything else going on. In particular, notice that you are having fun and are in a great mood. Add lots of color. Make the picture brighter, and bring it closer. When you've got the scene vividly in your mind, step into the picture so that you are no longer seeing it as a movie but experiencing it as you did when it happened. Hear the sounds, smell the smells, feel the sensations. What are you feeling? Since this is your fantasy which you will use to prepare for the future, you are free to make any changes you like. If you are dissatisfied or uncomfortable with any part of the experience, change it until it feels right.

Now "rewind" the memory tape to before the event. If you have any difficulty doing this, hold your head up, close your eyes, and start with a small part of the picture until you can build a complete scene. Then, make it move with action and add sound. Exactly what did you do to prepare? Remember as many details in sequence as you can. You may slow down the tape if necessary. Relive and re-enjoy how you prepared. What were you doing? How were you feeling? What, if anything, did you anticipate? What were your surroundings? Did you use any objects or "props" to put you in the mood? Was there music? Let yourself really enjoy the experience and when you're satisfied that you have extracted the important details from it, open your eyes and write down all the things you did to prepare to have fun.

Shelly, a self-employed interior designer, carefully works on her own "interior" before going out. She begins by asking herself, "What will make me feel really good?" As she begins to answer that question, she sometimes is reminded of problems and issues in her life that might get in the way of her good time. "One time," she recalls, "I was getting ready to go out and a financial worry was clouding my mind. I knew I couldn't handle it then and there, but I also knew if I didn't do something, I would be thinking of it all night. I remembered an exercise I had read about once for separating yourself from a problem. First, I made a commitment to myself to handle it first thing Monday morning. Then I visualized the problem and projected it on the wall. I put some music on and danced away from it." Other people write problems down on a sheet of paper or put them on their calendar to be handled later.

Once she felt no longer bothered by the problem, Shelly made it her mission to pamper herself. "I used to feel very uncomfortable and embarrassed about indulging myself in things like do-nothing afternoons and long baths. But when I go out to meet people now, I find it reassuring that I can make myself feel good. That allows me to choose people and situations more carefully. So I usually begin with the right music. If I am going dancing, I start the party early by playing some dance music. If something else is planned, I usually like quiet music. I also just enjoy being in my apartment, noticing the colors and the plants and the view out of the window. I find all of that very relaxing.

"I also make sure my clothing is appropriate, and that I feel really, really good wearing whatever I'm wearing. I've learned from experience that when I wear something uncomfortable or something that doesn't fit right, I'm distracted from having a good time. Before I leave, I make sure I have enough time to just sit quietly and remember all of my positive qualities. The times I've remembered to do this just before I arrive at the get-together, people have told me how good I look."

Other people like to involve their friends in their preparation routine. Sandy says: "One of the most enjoyable things about having a dance party is making the tapes beforehand. A week or so before the party, I usually invite a few friends over to help me make the selections. By the time the evening is over, we're so excited about the party, we can hardly stand it!"

Matthew likes to prepare for meeting new people by going out to dinner with a buddy. "It puts me in a relaxed frame of mind just talking and kidding with a close friend," he says. "We tend to energize each other, and by the time we get there, we're having so much fun that it seems we naturally draw people to us." If planning or preparing for an activity seems like a chore instead of a good time, invite a friend or two to share the experience with you. Whether you're waxing your skis, deciding what to pack for a camping trip, rehearsing for a musical, or practicing for a foreign language class, you can make preparing more fun by inviting other people to prepare with you.

Perhaps some of the things we've suggested sounded good to you, and you feel like you might want to try them out. Here are some other ideas to consider to help you refresh and renew yourself, and put yourself into the right mood for venturing out.

MENU OF PREPARATION ACTIVITIES

Do yoga, meditate, or do a relaxation exercise.

Humor yourself—watch reruns of your favorite situation comedy on TV. Listen to your comedy albums. Read a cartoon book. This is an excellent way to get out of the work mood and into the play mode.

Invite a friend over and prepare together. Get a massage.

Look at your social agenda and visualize what it will be like to have it fulfilled.

Go for a relaxing walk in the park, through the woods, or by the beach. Take your favorite dog with you, or find a new dog to play with.

Indulge yourself in one of your favorite activities.

Jog, run, workout, do anything that makes your body feel good.

Read passages from your favorite book, or read something that will improve your mood and self-esteem.

Spend time in your favorite corner of the house or under your favorite tree.

Take a relaxing hot bath.

Take a long, languid nap.

Unplug the phone and do absolutely nothing.

TIPS FOR CREATING YOUR
POSITIVE PREPARATION ROUTINE

1. Leave the stresses and strains of the workday behind. If something is bothering you that's likely to interfere with your good time, handle it now or make plans to handle it in the near future.

2. Make sure you're looking forward to a good time. Remind yourself that a good time is not contingent on meeting "the perfect person."

3. Load up on pleasant memories, fun activities, and positive experiences. Make mental movies of your greatest times and play these movies in your head before going out.

4. Design your own positive preparation routine. Make sure you start the fun early—do whatever it takes to make YOU feel good, relax, and prepare for fun.

5. Refer regularly to your list of "positive preparation activities." Ask your friends what they do to prepare. If you like what you hear, add them to your list—and to your repertoire.

6. Make the preparation phase an important and enjoyable part of your social life. Remember the purpose of the preparation is enjoyment, now as well as later.

7. Every moment of every day is part of your preparation process. Everything you do for yourself that enhances your self-esteem or your enjoyment of life goes into your "positive preparation treasure chest." Good times are cumulative, so stack them up like pancakes.

By now you have some ideas about turning around the negative thoughts that interfere with your good time, and replacing these with success attitudes. You also know how to design your environment to make you feel great. And you know how to use past successful experiences to project success into the future. To see what all of this looks like when it's put together, let's look at how Margaret designed a positive preparation routine that worked.

Margaret had always felt anxiety about throwing parties. She was afraid things wouldn't go well, or that other people wouldn't have a good time, or that for some other reason, the party would be "wrong." So she would rehearse these fears over and over—until they materialized. The tension she felt around the party would be picked up by everyone else involved. The result? A carefully rehearsed, self-fulfilling negative prophecy. A friend of Margaret's, Beth, asked her to co-host a party, and once again the old anxieties came up. But this time, Margaret decided to try something different.

As soon as Margaret began to feel apprehensive about the party, she replaced the feeling with what she wanted to feel. "I really wanted to enjoy the people who were coming," she says, "so I began by picturing myself looking fine, relaxed, and at ease. I saw myself wearing the dress I knew I'd be wearing, I saw myself greeting people at the door, glad to see them and enjoying them. I heard the sounds of the music and the chatter, and I genuinely felt the pleasure of having created this event."

Several times in the weeks before the party, Margaret felt the familiar feeling of apprehension sweep over her. Each time, she gently "changed the channel" to her own pictures of comfort and enjoyment. She did this at least half a dozen times, and each time it took only a minute to bring her mood back to one of positive anticipation. Whenever she found herself rehearsing for a "tragedy," she simply changed the play to a light, good-time comedy. Her preparation had another benefit as well—because she was feeling good about the party in general, she gave herself time to prepare her house and herself. The time before the party was relaxed, not hectic.

As part of her plan, Margaret took all the time she needed to prepare herself and get ready. "I set up my own mood and attitude and prepared myself to have a good time." First, she went through the house, making sure everything was the way she wanted it to look. Each time she felt the pressure of time, she reminded herself there was plenty of time to prepare. When she felt her enthusiasm flag for a moment, she called her friend Beth for some moral support. She made sure there was time to take a long, relaxing bath. After she dressed, she put on her favorite music. "I was sure to pick the records I associate with good times. It was the first time I actually enjoyed preparing. Now I find I enjoy the process so much, it doesn't matter how long it takes. The longer the better."

Margaret was even prepared to go into her "ideal party" space if she needed to once the party began—but she never needed to. "Once people began arriving," she says, "it no longer occurred to me to be uptight. I enjoyed everything that happened, and was totally delighted to be giving a party." She was so busy enjoying herself, that she had no time to waste worrying about whether everyone else was having a good time. Her hostess function was at a minimum. What she did, she did by example—and her example was, "Have a good time." She spent the evening greeting old friends, talking with new ones, dancing, and enjoying the energy of a good party. "I felt very attractive to people, especially a few of the men," she says. "I guess I would have to describe the feeling as gratifying and enlightening. The funny thing is, I had the feeling anything could have happened and it would have been all right."

As we said earlier, we are always rehearsing the future, one way or the other. When we allow ourselves to become immobilized with fear or anxiety, when we jump to conclusions such as: we won't know anybody there, no one will be interested in us, etc., we are preparing negatively. We are rehearsing failure. Notice that Margaret had many opportunities to rehearse failure. Each time she felt anxious about whether or not her guests would enjoy themselves, she could have turned that feeling into a mountain of distress. Instead, she gently reminded herself of what she wanted to happen—and pictured it happening. She saw her guests laughing, dancing, having a great time. And she put herself into this picture completely. Not only did she see this happening, but she herself was in it. She heard the music and laughter, she smelled the food, she felt the electricity of the party, and she felt a warm feeling inside. In effect, she created for herself a great party inside, and it became so real to her that she created it outside as well.

Remember that when you rehearse feeling good, you can take that feeling with you regardless of the circumstances you find yourself in. As Margaret remarked, she felt so good it almost didn't matter what happened at the party.

And finally, remember that developing a successful preparation routine is an ongoing learning process. As in any other learning process, whether it be playing guitar, riding a bike, learning French, or skiing, regular, repeated practice will increase your skill and eventually lead to success. There's no need to "try" or to be concerned that things are not happening quickly enough. Just as a house is built one brick at a time, so your positive preparation routine is improved one step at a time. Don't mistake the anxiety that comes with learning something new for evidence that meeting people is "impossible." Make a commitment to prepare yourself consciously for a few months, and you will find that meeting people will become second nature. It is amazing how discomfort can fade once you've learned new information and behavior. Most important of all, START NOW! The sooner you put this material to work for you, the sooner you will feel those positive results.

Chapter 11

Making contact doing what you love to do

Alice loves auto racing. She was about to watch the Indy 500 on TV when she thought better of it. She called a woman friend and together they went to watch the race at a local bar. "I figured I might as well turn it into a social event," she says. "I ended up meeting a lot of men who were surprised that I knew so much about racing. There was a lot of kidding and joking, and I noticed this one guy who was kind of quiet, but we kept making eye contact. During a commercial, I moved near him and he started a conversation. Even as I was being rowdy and circulating, I still sort of 'checked in' with him every now and then. After the race, we just naturally gravitated toward each other, and we ended up going out for a snack and talking. And we found we had a lot of other things in common as well."

Jeff, who signed up for an aerobics dance class because, "I find running boring, I love dance music, and I wanted to try something completely different for me," relates this story of how he met a new friend: "When I got to the class and discovered there were only a few guys, I felt extremely uncomfortable and self-conscious. The first class I concentrated on keeping up with the steps, which I found really challenging. I was still pretty self-conscious the second class, but I found it a little more enjoyable this time. I also noticed this woman in the class, and we made eye contact once or twice. On the way out of class the third week, she said to me, 'You mean to tell me you haven't dropped out of the class yet?' I looked at her funny, and she told me that men usually drop out pretty quickly. I told her I'd never drop out, and we were off! As we talked, we discovered a common interest in theater, so that was a source of another whole conversation. After that, it was easy for me to invite her out to coffee."

"I met the man I've been dating at a party for people in the bike touring club I belong to," says Laura. "Everyone was dancing up a storm and having fun. I had been there for an hour or more, and found myself in one room where people were just milling around. I was taking a breather, when I looked around and noticed this man standing there. We looked at each other, and I just said, 'Hi' and smiled, and he said 'Hi' and smiled back. I liked the fact that there was no introduction. We just sort of bumped into each other and started talking. I think we both thought, this looks like an interesting person, so we decided to check each other out.

"We had really good rapport as we talked and found out we had the same kind of jobs and knew a lot of people in common. We talked for a while and then I felt it was time to move on and see some other people and he went and did something else as well. At various times in the evening, we talked again and went our separate ways. That felt very relaxed and natural, and I enjoy that. We ended up dancing, and we were among the last people to leave. Our cars happened to be parked around the corner from each other, and we found that we each had these beat-up old foreign cars—like everything else, we had that in common also. While we were laughing about our cars, he asked me if I wanted to play squash sometime. I had never played squash before, but I said sure. We played squash the following Saturday night and we've been going out ever since."

Dave, new in town, decided to join a softball team as a way to have fun and meet people. "I didn't know anyone on the team, I just signed up as an extra player. Luckily, it turned out to be a fun-loving group, and we gave each other lots of encouragement. I just seemed to gravitate toward this one guy, Phil, because he also had an East Coast accent. It turned out that we were both from New York—he was from Brooklyn, I was from the Bronx—and we decided we needed to bring stickball to the Midwest. So we ended up starting our own little stickball league, and we've had a lot of good times and turned a lot of our new friends on to an old city sport."

Georgia met the woman who would become her best friend on an archeological dig. Says Georgia, "I've always been fascinated with archeology, and this dig was lots of fun, and also lots of work—a lot of dust and drudgery. This woman in our group made a funny comment one time, and I responded and pretty soon we were laughing and joking all the time. It seemed that all we had to do was look at each other, and we'd crack up. I don't know why. I decided that I would make sure to stay in touch with her when we got back to the city because no matter what we did, I knew we'd have fun."

In talking with people about how they met significant people in their lives, we heard the same kinds of stories over and over again. People met close friends and dating partners most frequently while absorbed in an activity they enjoyed. Fun activity, it seems, creates a natural bridge for contact to be made and sustained. The activity creates a pleasurable glow and allows you to observe and make eye contact with someone several times before you actually speak to one another. This repeated contact in the course of the activity creates trust and familiarity, so it's easy to smile, walk over and speak to someone without feeling intrusive or self-conscious. When you do speak to one another, the activity itself is an excellent conversation starter and a way to build rapport. Finally, when you've used the conversation to determine each other's interests it's a natural step to invite the other person to do one of these fun activities in the future.

Of course, you may look at your own life and find exceptions to this pattern. But you will probably find that more often than not, your most successful meetings involved fun, activity, proximity, repeated contact, rapport, and follow-up. You may also notice that there is a certain degree of luck or chance involved in meeting people. But as the saying goes, "Luck is where preparation and opportunity meet." If you prepare well and you go to the places where you are most likely to find the opportunities you are looking for, you can stack the odds in your favor.

You decide for yourself what "success" is in a social setting. It may be saying hello to a number of new people. It may be getting the phone number of one or more potential friends. It may be building friendships with people you have recently met. Or it

might be simply getting used to social situations again. Whatever
your goals, keep in mind two things. If at any time in the people-
meeting process you feel pressured or mistreated, move away, at
least temporarily. And if there's someone or some activity you want
to check out, you are free to gracefully excuse yourself and go do
that. Even if you feel uncomfortable at first, you will find it easier
and easier to move toward what you want and away from what you
don't want. And the more you move through social settings pursuing your own social agenda, the more meeting people will feel like
the fun adventure it is.

KEY 25

"If the idea of meeting people leaves you cold, warm up first by moving around and noticing where the fun is."

Has this ever happened to you? You get invited to a social
get-together where you don't know very many people. Since you're
determined to meet new friends, you decide to go—reluctantly.
Once you get there, you realize you've made a dreadful mistake. Everybody knows everybody else—except for you. So you find yourself a little piece of floor near the potato chips, and you stand there
frozen for most of the evening. And you never quite get thawed out.
A few people say a word or two to you, but you feel so cold and stiff
to them, that they move on quickly. Others mistake you for a coat
rack. That's when you decide it's time to go home.

Just as the professional tennis player would never dream
of playing a match without warming up, you cannot expect to play
the people-meeting game unless you warm up to your surroundings. The athlete will warm up by moving around and stretching his
muscles through their full range of motion. In the same way, you
can warm up to a social setting by moving around so that you feel at
home anywhere in the room. Not only does this give you a full range
of "social motion," but it puts you in the proper mood as you notice
people and activities you want to check out further. Whether you
are off to a theater opening, a lecture, a barbecue, or any other so-

cial gathering, try making at least two "tours" before settling into a conversation or activity.

The first tour we call the "Lewis & Clark Tour." You are an explorer, and your mission is to scope out every inch of the territory. This will give you a sense of who's there that you would like to meet, which activities you want to try, where the beer is, where the punch is, where the chips are. By simply walking through the place and noticing what's going on where, you will be able to return to any part of the territory comfortably. You will find yourself warming up—literally—as you begin anticipating and planning how you might spend your day or evening.

This tour will serve another important function. It will help you decide whether you want to stay or leave. Perhaps there's really no one there you want to meet, or there is something going on that you don't enjoy. You were expecting an astronomy lecture, and this is astrology? People are ingesting strange drugs and preparing huge vats of Jell-O (and you hate Jell-O)? A motorcycle gang has taken over the living room—with their motorcycles? You already know everyone there, and you're bored to tears by them? After you complete your tour, ask yourself, "Is this a place where I can meet the kind of people I want to meet and have a great time?" If there are few or no new people at the event, ask yourself, "Is it early enough so that more people are likely to show up? Can I use this gathering to firm up old acquaintances and find out about new social settings?" "Is the activity or event so much fun that I want to stay, even if it isn't likely that I'll be able to pursue my social agenda?" If the answer to these questions is no, by all means leave. Thank the host or hostess or the person who invited you and be on your way. You are under no obligation to put in time being with people you don't want to be with doing things you don't enjoy. Socializing is supposed to be fun. Leave obligations for things like work. A negative social experience can dampen your enthusiasm for going out in the future. On the other hand, once you realize you can always leave if it's not for you, you will be less likely to hesitate to try out new things. Before you do leave, however, make sure you are not leaving for the wrong reasons. Take a moment to notice if your attitude is getting in the way of having fun. Are you jumping to conclusions about people? Making an unwarranted association with a past unpleasant experience? Do you need to do something to turn your mood around? Or are you just apprehensive about a new social situation? If you feel driven to leave because you're intimidated by all of the interesting people you might meet, put your coat away NOW! You just need to warm up a little more.

Assuming Lewis & Clark noticed some potential fun and interesting new people, it's time to take tour number two. We call this the "Glenn Miller Tour" because it helps you get "in the mood." Before embarking on this second tour, take your "temperature." Are you completely thawed? Are your people-meeting muscles loose? Are you feeling a warm glow that expresses itself as a smile? On this Glenn Miller Tour, you will be doing whatever is necessary to warm up to "room temperature"—and beyond. As you walk around this time, notice some of the specific things you would like to do and people you would like to meet. Imagine yourself involved in the activities you see and the conversations you hear. Remember times when you were in a similar setting and had a great time meeting people, and picture some of those pleasant times happening again in this new setting. Bring your attention back to your Positive Preparation Routine and think of the fun you anticipated. It is that sense of fun and pleasure that you take with you and project outward as you move through the social setting. By all means, smile and say "hello" to the people you come in contact with. The early "hello" or "how-are-you-doing" or any other simple, friendly greeting will make it much easier to talk with those people later on in the event. And the smiles you receive will warm you even more.

Of course, not every setting will be conducive to wandering around. Let's say you find yourself seated at a concert, at a lecture, or lined up waiting to tour a museum or step into the planetarium. You can still take a visual tour by noticing your surroundings—particularly the other people—and allowing yourself to feel comfortable, relaxed, and at home. Particularly if you tend to be shy in new situations, take all the time you need to warm up. During this Glenn Miller Tour you need not do anything more than move around and observe other people. You will find that the more you focus on what's really going on out there, the less you will be conscious of your own butterflies and what people might be thinking about you. Not only will you become curious about other people, but you will pick up bits of conversation and notice things that you can use to make contact later. Most people are too busy worrying about what others think about them to really look and listen. Take the time to do that, immerse yourself in the pre-glow of fun activity, and you'll be way ahead. You'll be more confident in yourself because you will know more about what makes others tick. And you'll realize that other people are just as nervous as you are! If you find yourself absorbed in the conversation that's going on inside your head, focus your attention on the conversations out there instead.

As you take this second tour, "try things on" in your

imagination. Taste and test. Picture yourself IN the volleyball game, ON the dance floor, AT the poolside, ABSORBED in the discussion. Step into the pictures and see what it feels like to be in those activities. Remind yourself of your agenda, and think about what you would like to experience during this social event. Be realistic in your expectations—while it might be great to meet the love of your life, don't make your good time contingent on meeting that person. Move away from the chill of pressure to "find somebody," and toward the warm glow of fun. Choose experiences where you can have some control over the outcome. For example:

1. Talk to at least two new people, even it it's just saying hello.
2. Dance, either with an old acquaintance or a new friend.
3. Feel confident and attractive.
4. Move around rather than become a piece of furniture stuck in one area.
5. Join in at least one activity you really enjoy.
6. Introduce yourself to someone you've never met but have heard a lot about.
7. Collect the names of at least two people you'd like to invite to future activities.
8. Excuse yourself comfortably and gracefully and move on to someone or something else.

Observing and planning your day or evening are important steps, but don't spend the entire time touring! If you've completed the Glenn Miller Tour and you're still feeling a bit of a chill, this is a signal that you need to get more active.

KEY 26

" Active molecules have the most chemical interactions. "

If you're hoping to create chemistry with someone at this event, you must first make contact with people. And you can increase your chances for contact by being active. As you may remember from high school, those molecules that are the most active get into the most chemical interactions. So if you still aren't warm yet, notice if you're hanging back like an inert gas. If you are, consider taking a third tour, what we call the "Old Time Religion Tour" because you're "on a mission." And your mission is to make eye contact, smile, and say hello to a number of people. If the story you tell yourself is "No one notices me," take this opportunity to be noticeable and get noticed.

If it suits your mood, find yourself a more formal "mission." Offer to hang up the coats, pour the punch, direct traffic, collect the tickets. Be sure the role is temporary, however, and doesn't deprive you of enjoying the rest of the event. Sarah told us that one of her most enjoyable times was when she was taking tickets at a dance. "I was able to meet and greet everyone as they were coming in. It was a great opportunity to kibitz with people, and put me in the right frame of mind. By the time the event started, I felt as if I knew half the people in the room. I even felt comfortable asking a few of the guys to dance, because I had talked with them earlier."

Place yourself in the thick of things, where the fun is. The more you make yourself part of any event, the more likely others are to walk up to you and ask you what is happening. Get involved, and you'll give off an air of self-assurance. Also, you'll be too busy with your role to be self-conscious. Most important, you will be noticed. As you meet people, play the game of remembering their names. Each time you get introduced to someone, take a moment to picture his name emblazoned on his forehead in some bright color like red or orange. People love it when you remember their names, and it makes the second contact easier. And they'll remember you as the person who gave their forehead a funny look when they told you their name.

The single most important element of successful contact is also the most obvious—proximity. Whom are we most likely to get to know—and even fall in love with? The people we see time after time, day after day! Statistics prove we tend to become friends with and marry people we grow up with, go to school with, work with, go to church with, ride the bus with. We are close to these people and we get to know them over time. This applies in every social setting. The people we end up creating chemistry with are those who are in proximity. We create proximity by standing near or sitting near people, sharing an activity with them, or by making eye contact with them, even if they are across the room. The more frequently we are in proximity with someone, the better the chances of sustaining contact.

By far the most comfortable way of being closer is through shared activity. When you're swimming together, or playing charades, or standing around in a group at intermission, you are automatically in proximity. There's no excuse needed for contact. And the activity itself is the focus of attention and the natural object of conversation. Contrast this with a setting where you must get up, walk over to someone, and initiate a conversation out of the clear blue—or wait for someone to approach you.

"The reason I love square dancing," Charles says, "is that some of the dances allow you to switch partners frequently. I really enjoy noticing how a new person responds to me, and how I feel about her. If there's a special smile or electricity, it's the easiest thing in the world to ask her for the next dance or chat during a break. It's a whole lot easier than walking across the room to ask a total stranger to dance." Other people told us they enjoy small, interactive classes (e.g., cooking or photography) or discussion groups where participants face each other. Trivial Pursuit, charades, and board games are also excellent ways to talk, laugh, participate with others—and have a conversation naturally emerge from the fun of the activity.

Mary and two of her girlfriends were waiting outside a club to hear some music. Already caught up in the excitement of the coming event, it was easy for them to joke and talk with the group of guys standing next to them. "Once we got inside," Mary says, "it was just the most natural thing for us to sit at the same table. The guys we met saved us a place at their table, and before I knew it I was engrossed in a conversation with one of them. And that's how I met my husband."

But suppose, at a larger event or social gathering you see someone you'd like to meet—only that probably won't happen in the natural course of events. What do you do then? Even if you don't feel comfortable enough to walk up to them, take the smaller step of putting yourself in proximity. By doing this, you increase the chances that they notice you, and you increase the chances of conversation. Janet reports that at a party, she noticed a man who looked interesting. "I could never have walked up to him and introduced myself," she says, "so I decided to stand near him and see if he said anything to me. Sure enough, he made a friendly comment, I responded, and we were off and running."

KEY 27

" Place yourself near the person you'd like to meet. "

Not only does moving closer increase the chances of contact, but it also puts you in a better position to observe and listen to that person. One of the biggest obstacles to making contact with people is fear of being misunderstood or rejected. You can't really control how people will respond to you, but by careful observation you can improve your chances of finding someone who might be interested. Are you feeling nervous or self-conscious? Turn that sensitivity to your advantage and focus it outward, toward the person you are curious about. What do you find attractive or interesting about this person? Does he or she seem friendly? Aloof? Interested? Bored? If this person is conversing with someone else, does it seem to you like they're intimate friends? New acquaintances? Do they seem ready to end the conversation or does it look like they have made a strong connection? Notice their posture. Does it seem open? Inviting? Defensive? What does their facial expression tell you? A number of books have been written about "body language" and what various body cues mean. Most people have the ability to "speak" and "read" this body language, provided they take the time to observe. The best way to learn to read body language is to experiment. Follow your hunches, then notice whether you were right. That way, if you make a mistake at least you've done it in the name of science.

You'll get a better sense of whether a person is really approachable at that moment if you allow yourself to hear bits of the conversation. Is it idle chatter or a budding romance? Why guess when you can find out by moving a little closer? You might also pick up interesting tidbits which you can use later on to initiate conversation with that person. When you find yourself sitting next to that person or waiting in line for the restroom, you can say, "I heard you mention that you're a teacher. So am I." This is perfectly acceptable, by the way, and happens all the time. People are usually flattered that you cared enough to listen. Beware, however, of conversation openers like, "I couldn't help but overhear that you've just gotten a divorce," or other obviously personal information. There is a significant difference between overhearing casual conversation and eavesdropping on a confidential discussion.

Sometimes you can interject yourself into a conversation when someone has raised a question and no one seems to know the answer. At a party, Jennifer was standing near a group of people who were discussing architecture. She overheard someone mention a Frank Lloyd Wright house in town, but no one seemed to know where it was located. Jennifer found easy entry into the conversation by letting the group know exactly where the house was. Says Jennifer, "I immediately was accepted into the conversation and when the group split up to refill their glasses, I found myself talking with a man I had been wanting to meet the entire evening. The whole thing happened so naturally I forgot to be nervous."

So . . . you've been watching and listening to an interesting person now for about five minutes. You yearn to go up and talk to her, but some fear seems to be holding you back. Your mind begins playing back countless experiences of real or imagined rejections, and the warm mood you've been feeling is rapidly turning into cold feet. "I knew this meeting-people stuff wasn't for me," you say to yourself. "This always happens!" Unless something happens to change your mood, you are likely to ruin your evening.

If that has happened to you in the past, the chances are good it can happen again even if you have prepared your mood and warmed up carefully. Fortunately, there are a number of things you can do.

1. RELAX AND BREATHE.   Just the simple act of taking a deep breath, and consciously relaxing the muscles of your body can turn your mood from cold apprehension to heated anticipation. One thing that will help you relax is "lowering the stakes." Instead of thinking that the person you want to meet is a potential date or mate, remind yourself that he or she is simply someone you might like to get to know.

2. CHANGE THE CHANNEL.   If you find yourself dwelling on past negative experiences, change the picture to a time when you were having a great time meeting people. If no incident comes to mind, make one up! Make the picture bright and vivid and add as much pleasure as you can stand. At the first sign of being nervous, Laura began replaying an experience she had at a concert a few months earlier. "I must have been totally immersed in reliving the event," she says, "because this guy walked up to me and asked what I was smiling about. We started talking, and it turned out he had been to the same concert!"

3. BE APPROACHABLE.   If it's too big a step to approach someone else, you can at least be approachable. An open look, a smile, relaxed posture, all go a long way to letting people know that you don't bite. Allow yourself to look at people you are interested in for a few seconds more than at other people. You might be surprised to find them walking over and talking to you!

4. MAKE EYE CONTACT.   The thought of going up and asking a perfect stranger to dance may leave you utterly cold. One way around this is to make eye contact with the person first. Says Roy, "I find it intimidating to just ask a woman to dance, and I don't know how other guys can just go up and do it cold. What I try to do is make eye contact, not once but several times. I put myself in her sights, so to speak, so that she can have a chance to see me and feel comfortable with me. Sometimes we end up smiling at each other. That way, when I approach her, I feel like I'm approaching someone I already know."

5. GO TOWARD THE FUN.   If you're feeling stuck, get moving! Go dance, get some chips, joke with some friends. Whatever it is that's the most fun for you at this event, go do it. Chances are, you will meet people while you are immersed in this activity. Melanie says, "I was at a picnic, and I noticed a guy I really wanted to meet. I didn't know how to approach him, and I felt really nervous. Finally, I decided to go play volleyball. Who do you think ended up joining my team? We had a great time, and it was really easy to start up a conversation after that."

What about just walking up to people, introducing yourself, and starting a conversation? "The thought of just walking up to someone and talking used to paralyze me," Walt admits. "One time at a party I was feeling a bit daring and playful, so I turned to a woman next to me and asked if she'd heard any good jokes lately. She was a little taken aback, so I offered to tell her one. That got the ball rolling. Since then, I've started dozens of conversations that way with sales clerks, at parties, at the movies, just on the street. You'd be surprised how well people respond. And those few times when people just looked at me funny and didn't answer, I figured I didn't want to meet those people anyway."

Walt discovered that many people who like jokes don't

necessarily think of themselves as good joke-tellers. To take the pressure off the situation, Walt will offer to tell them a joke first. "I always make sure it's a really dumb joke," he says. "That gives them permission to be silly and not have to worry whether they're coming across like a professional comedian or not. I've heard a lot of my favorite jokes that way, and I've met a lot of new people."

Even if telling jokes is not your thing, you can still approach people in a playful manner. A sociologist friend of ours used to present new acquaintances with a card that announced his profession as "Refrigerologist." He would then explain that he could tell people all about themselves just by looking in their refrigerators. He had a lot of interesting conversations this way, and got to see a few refrigerators, as well. Whatever playful gambit you use, make sure it's appropriate for you and the situation. Even if you're naturally reserved and reluctant to walk up to a new person, keep in mind that you have very little to lose. Time and time again people have told us that if they're approached genuinely and politely, they themselves will be polite and friendly, even if they're not interested in a long conversation.

One of the easiest ways to open a conversation is to make an observation or ask an open-ended question about the activity you just shared or the environment in general. These are safe subjects since they allow the two of you to focus on something "out there" rather than begin a conversation on an overly personal, probing note. Open-ended questions ("What did you think of the last speaker?") are better than those that can be answered yes or no ("Do you like the carob-tofu dip?") because they invite further discussion. To make the best first impression, be genuine and be positive. A genuine statement will elicit enthusiasm; phoniness can be smelled a mile away. If you are extraordinarily impressed with how awful the band is and have a strong sense the person standing next to you feels the same way, say so. But the sooner you steer the conversation to music you do like, the more chance you'll have of establishing positive rapport. Beware, however, of pointing to a fellow at the next table and asking a new acquaintance, "Hey, is that a tie or a chest-protector or what?" She might very well icily reply that the man happens to be her brother and the tie is one she gave him for Christmas.

You can also use people's appearances, something they are carrying or wearing, or something that you overheard to initiate conversation. Examples include: "Are those African earrings?" "That sounds like a New England accent to me. Is it?" "I overheard you say you grew up in Indiana. So did I." If you choose to point out a personal attribute, and particularly if you are complimenting the person, make sure the interest and compliment are genuine. Our friend Laura says her guideline for giving compliments is as follows: If the thought naturally and of its own accord occurs to you that you like something about someone, say it. It's those contrived compliments that project phoniness and turn people off.

Like it or not, we all tend to make initial judgments about people based on how they look. We also may decide that we like or dislike them by the way they speak. Next time you're at a social gathering, take a few minutes and just listen to voices without noticing who is speaking. Notice how you feel around different voices. People are not always aware of how their voices can attract people or turn them off. How does your voice sound to a stranger? Is it harsh or abrasive? Throaty? Sexy? High-pitched? Too soft and meek? Do you speak without breathing? Talk too fast? Too slowly? Too much? The more comfortable you are with yourself, the more likely you are to be using the voice that will attract the people you want to attract.

In the first few moments of contact, we are taking people in with all of our senses. What smells do you find attractive, which turn you off? How do you come across in the olfactory department? Are you overladen with perfume or after shave? Or do you project a little too much natural aroma? Keep in mind that individual preferences vary, although both of the extremes are likely to be turn-offs for a lot of people. Do you touch people appropriately? Or are you premature with it, or invasive? Touch is like a delicate spice which should be used only at the right moments. In the initial stages of contact, touch should be nothing more than a handshake or a light touch on the hand or shoulder—and only if you are sure the other person will be comfortable with that. If you feel the person is not yet comfortable, stay in her line of vision and don't touch her until you've gotten a signal that she's invited you to do so. When in doubt, wait until she's come forward and touched you first!

Women particularly find premature touch a turn-off. Margaret says she was put off by a man she was introduced to at a party who immediately hugged her and called her "love." "I just wanted to leave as soon as I could," she says. "I felt socially violated and trapped, and I avoided being around him the rest of the evening. Whenever I meet anyone who invades my space like this guy, I find myself moving away. If I'm interested, I want to be the one to move closer."

The people we spoke with offered the following advice on what promotes and what inhibits successful contact.

CONTACT ENHANCERS

Active listening
A comment about shared fun activity
A direct approach, but not overly aggressive
A smile
Balanced conversation
Eye contact
Finding mutual interests, drawing the other person
    out
Genuine compliments
Having a good time
Kempt appearance, healthy look
Liveliness, playfulness
Looking approachable
Pleasant voice
Relaxed, genial manner
Respect for personal and emotional space
Sensitivity to the other person's rhythm, pace, mood
Sense of humor
Showing genuine interest in the other person

CONTACT STOPPERS

Bitching, complaining, putting others down
Boastfulness, arrogance, one-upmanship
Boredom
Cigarette smoking
Drunkenness
Flattery
Getting too familiar too quickly
Gloominess
Invasion of comfort zone
Irritating voice
Obscenity
Overdressed or over-sloppy appearance
Pretentiousness
Roving eye, indirect look
Silliness, immature behavior
Spilling out entire life story in first three minutes
The "puppy dog" attitude—following you around
Tired lines, obvious come-ons, double entendre clichés
Trying too hard

Most of the people we spoke with—men and women alike—agreed they are attracted by smiles, self-confidence, and genuine interest in getting to know them as a person. People most commonly listed as turn-offs bragging, gloominess, insincerity, and tired "lines." "Those clever come-on lines that sound so good in the movies," George says, "work so badly in real life." Of course, a well-placed clever line can create a playful mood and lead to rapport. Put-downs and sexual innuendos seldom work, however. Playfulness can be a turn-on but it can easily cross the border into silliness and offensiveness—so check your border patrol. Dave reports that he once met a woman at a party by playfully putting ice down her back. The second time he tried that, the results were less positive. "I got so carried away that I didn't notice she wasn't enjoying it as much as I was," he admits. Dave ended up breaking the woman's gold necklace, and he saw his name permanently erased from this woman's desirables list.

Keep in mind that even the most gallant, sensitive, pleasant person is not going to hit it off with everyone. What may feel like a turn-down or a rejection may have nothing whatever to do with you. Ask what you can learn from any seemingly unsuccessful encounter. Was the person really approachable? Did you go for too large an outcome too quickly (e.g., ask a perfect stranger to dance without first making eye contact)? Did you make contact in a way that allowed the other person to respond comfortably? A woman who attended one of our seminars told us she no longer asked men to dance because of a rebuff she received a few months earlier. When we asked how she approached the man, she said, "I walked up to him and said, 'Do you dance or do you just stand there and look gorgeous?' " Apparently, this line was a bit too overwhelming for the man, and he replied coldly, "I just stand here and look gorgeous." The woman was crushed. She had gone for the big splash but hadn't checked to see if the pool had been filled.

If you found yourself outside a clique of friends who seemed to be ignoring your wanting to be included, don't take this as a personal rejection. Have you ever been in a situation where you were with a group of people you knew well, joking and talking about things that had meaning for just your group? It's very easy to get absorbed in this in-group and forget there are other people around. It's also important that you realize that not all people have meeting new friends on their agendas. Just as you would like others to be sensitive to your wanting to be included, be sensitive to their desire to be with old friends.

Remember that the more you initiate contact, the easier it

gets. And the more you learn about how to do it the next time. Make it a point to initiate conversations with strangers in non-threatening situations, and you will find yourself making it an unconscious habit. Look at meeting people and making friends as an adventure, and you as a great explorer.

YOUR ACTION PLAN FOR MAKING CONTACT HAVING FUN

1. Remember that it is much easier to make contact while having fun, so prepare yourself to enjoy the activity or event.
2. Warm up by familiarizing yourself with the place. Be sure to smile and say hello to the people you meet along the way.
3. Immerse yourself in fun activity.
4. Notice the people you want to meet, look at them and smile.
5. Use the activity as a natural bridge to conversation.
6. Find out what the other person loves to do.

Making contact and initiating conversation is the first important step. In the next chapter, we'll have a look at how you can sustain contact long enough to know if the person you've met is someone you'd like to know.

Chapter 12

66Creating rapport99

      Once you have made contact with a person, the next step—assuming you want to get to know the person better—is to keep the contact going. Perhaps you've enjoyed dancing or swimming or skiing for a while and you're ready to take a breather. Or you're standing outside of the darkroom waiting to develop your photos. Or maybe you've been part of a group conversation and you now find yourself talking with just one person. Or you've just walked up and introduced yourself to someone. How do you let him know what you're about and find out who he is?

      Conversation is the natural way to get to know someone, and almost any question or comment can be used to spark a conversation: "I love this kind of music—what do you like?" "How did you hear about this party?" "I usually don't go to gallery openings, but this one seems like fun." And so on. The best conversation openers tend to focus on shared experience rather than on either one of the partners, and are either questions or comments that invite response. You're not trying to impress people with how wonderful you are or intimidate them into wanting to spend time with you. You're simply offering a "calling card" and gently knocking at their door to find out who's home. Remember that your intention here is not to seize upon new acquaintances, but to draw them in so that they move closer on their own accord. A warm smile and a gentle manner work far better than an aggressive attitude.

To establish rapport means to create comfort and trust. One way to establish trust is by finding common ground. You have already gone a long way in this direction if you've just shared an enjoyable activity. Having a friend in common with a new person will also help establish that you are "safe." Being part of the network will also increase the chances that you share common interests and values with that person. And of course, it will provide fuel for conversation. ("Oh, so you know Roger . . . Isn't he something? . . . How did you meet him? Did you know him when blah-blah-blah? . . .") Many people will begin conversations "scanning" for common references like school, career, hometown, friends, or hobbies. Questions are a good way to solidify contact, but make sure the conversation is balanced and you don't come off sounding like an interrogator.

You will notice that once you have established common ground, you will be able to feel increased excitement and interest. Jean reports that she was talking with a new acquaintance when the conversation turned to the outdoors. She told him that she had gone rafting on a particular river. It turned out that he had been kayaking on the same river. Since it had been an enjoyable and exciting experience for both of them, they had plenty of fuel for an animated conversation. Over the course of the evening, they found a number of things in common, and when he was ready to leave it was easy for Jean's new friend to extend an invitation: "The kayaking club is meeting on Saturday. Would you like to come check it out?"

Beware of the temptation towards one-upmanship, particularly when you're sharing similar experiences. When someone tells you she's been to twelve European countries, it's all too easy to respond that you've been to thirteen. As Dave told us, "If he says he flies a plane, don't tell him you fly a jet plane—for a living. Let the other person feel comfortable in his own realm of competence." It's also a good idea to leave a little silent space after the other person has finished talking. This will indicate that you have been listening, and will establish a balanced, relaxed rhythm to the conversation.

The people who are the best conversationalists are the ones who are interestED rather than interestING. Avoid too much talking about yourself. Even if other people do seem interested, keep the conversation in balance. Continue to find out who THEY are and they'll be impressed that someone as interesting as you is interested in them. "I already know about me," George says. "I want to find out about her."

Find out the things people want to reveal about themselves. Draw the other person out by asking questions, and listen attentively. Be sure to notice whether the questions are turning the person on or off. Margaret says, "If he turns into a zombie when you mention work, quickly change the subject to movies."

But don't get so lost in drawing other people out that you forget to let them know who YOU are. Whenever you meet a new person, you're bound to remind each other of people you already know or knew in the past. This can have both positive and negative implications. To distinguish yourself from the preconceptions and stereotypes that others may have about you, it's a good idea to let the other person know through your casual comments what is unique about you. Don Gabor, author of *How to Start a Conversation and Make Friends,* suggests that you volunteer "free information" about your interests, what you value in life, your life stage, background, or anything else that will set you apart. This doesn't mean that you recite your "life résumé" to new acquaintances, but rather that you offer tidbits about yourself in the natural flow of conversation. These can include comments about a particularly interesting book you've just read, a film you've seen, a fun adventure, or even something special that happened that day or that week. A casual comment can spark an animated conversation, and possibly a lifetime friendship.

KEY 28

" A great way to turn other people on is to get them talking about what turns them on. "

Even at social gatherings where the focus is not on activities, "love-to-dos" can be a bridge. "I was at a party," Stan told us, "and I was introduced to a woman I found attractive. Instead of doing what I normally do—asking, 'So what do you do?'—I impulsively asked, 'What do you really enjoy in life?' And she went right into describing how each year she gets involved with this 'medieval festival' where they dress up in medieval costumes, have contests and music and so on. I'd never even heard of these, but after talking with her for forty-five minutes, I was as excited about it as she was. Then she asked me what I loved to do—and we spent the rest of the evening talking. A year later, we were married."

Even if you don't end up marrying any of the people you ask, "What do you enjoy doing?" you will at least find out what they're like when they're turned on. Talking about what they enjoy will certainly put them in a positive frame of mind. And if you share their enthusiasm and genuinely enjoy hearing about their great times, they will associate you with those great times! On the other hand, if your conversation consists of comparing "ain't-it-awfuls," you may establish rapport, but when they want a good time they'll go elsewhere—to someone they've established a good-time rapport with. Finally, you will find out just what a person enjoys. Should you want to get together later, mutual interests will provide a strong bridge—as Jean discovered with her friend the kayaker. Make it a mission to find out what turns people on; as an advanced exercise, get someone to tell you his most outrageously great time.

Linda told us that she and a new acquaintance "laughed until they cried" comparing funny skiing adventures. "After that," she says, "we could talk about anything. We had revealed and laughed about some of our most embarrassing times. He ended up asking me to dance even though he said he rarely danced. He said he had nothing to lose since he had already told me what a klutz he was."

If you're not particularly turned on by the usual questions people ask one another, try something more playful. Charlie told us of playing "What's My Line?" with a new acquaintance. In the process of trying to guess each other's occupations, they found out a great deal about each other—and had a great time as well. They turned what could have been a boring recitation of facts into an exciting game. Another person we spoke with went to bars armed with a "psychological questionnaire" and got new acquaintances to answer the questions! Again, whatever playful way you use to try and get to know people, make sure they are appropriate for both you and the situation. Don't treat your new acquaintance like a guest on "Firing Line." Too many questions too fast can end the conversation before it begins.

There's more to good rapport than conversation. Rapport means looking and listening carefully to make sure that the person is still with you. One of the characteristics of the bore is that he (yes guys, it's often a "he") doesn't bother to find out if the other person is listening or even cares. He is in a closed-loop conversation with himself. The listener is just the prop.

Laura told us about the time she answered an ad for a roommate. "I liked the apartment," she says, "but the woman who I would have been sharing it with was a real turn-off. As soon as I walked in the door, her tape started running. There was a constant monologue about what SHE was looking for in a roommate, what SHE did for a living, how SHE liked the house kept. There was never a space in the conversation for me to say anything about myself. She didn't even ask. I felt that if I moved in, I'd be nothing more than a piece of furniture to her."

The best way to avoid being a bore is to focus at least half of your attention on the other person. Notice what the other person is telling you through his or her voice tone and body language. Does the other person seem interested? Or is he or she restlessly eyeing someone or something across the room? Notice the other person's speech patterns, posture, gestures. Are you in sync with the other person? Are you matching the other person's mood, or are you attempting to steamroll through with your agenda? The more closely your behavior and mood match that of your partner, the more likely you are to establish rapport. This doesn't mean that you become a human chameleon and hide your true self behind what you think the other person wants you to be. It means that you tune into the other person carefully, and be sure you're on the same channel.

What if you're involved in a conversation and the subject is one you are bored with or care little about? Let the other person know and suggest changing the subject: "You know, I'm really not that interested in the balance of payments. Let's find a topic we're both interested in." If your partner balks at this, it might be a good indication that it's time for you to move on.

TIPS FOR ESTABLISHING RAPPORT

1. Maintain eye contact. If you're talking to someone, look at her. This lets her know you are paying attention, and care about what she's saying. It also allows you to tune into her mood and respond appropriately. The people we spoke with agreed that one of the biggest turn-offs is the "roving eye" who is everywhere but with the person he or she is talking with.

2. Respect the personal space of others, and demand the same of them. An invasive approach, whether physical or verbal, is likely to drive the person to the other side of the room. Don't touch unless you receive an invitation. Judy says she enjoys men who "will stay at arm's length until I have reached out." Men, allow the woman to invite you to come closer by moving closer to you. Learn to watch for and respond to these subtle cues. Politeness and good manners build bridges. Obnoxious come-ons and obvious ploys for sex blow bridges up.

3. Beware of overwhelming the other person with too much attention too soon. "Sometimes it takes me a while to figure out how I feel about someone," said one of the women we spoke with. "If I feel I'm going to have a hard time setting limits with someone, I tend to shut down right away." Just as new acquaintances need physical space, they also need emotional space. If you follow people around like a lost puppy, chances are you will end up in their dog house—alone.

4. Learn to appreciate differences. Rapport is more than shared interests. Even if it doesn't exactly match yours, you may find someone else's world interesting and curious and fun to explore. Look for common ground with new acquaintances, but also celebrate and enjoy the differences as well.

5. Make sure the conversation is balanced. If you notice you have been talking nonstop for twenty minutes, take a breather. Apologize for hogging the conversation, and give the other person a chance in the spotlight. If you find yourself left out of the conversation and your attempts to speak thwarted, feel free to dismiss yourself—unless you've paid for a lecture.

6. Sometimes the best rapport is the silent kind. This is particularly true of dancing. Says Jeff, "One of the little games I play when dancing with a new person is to experiment with moving closer and moving further away. I also enjoy it when I get into another person's rhythm. I find I can pick up on her mood that way." Next time you're at a social gathering, be aware of how people physically respond to each other nonverbally by moving closer or further away, or by matching each other's posture and movements. Notice who seems to be in sync, and who is out of sync.

7. Avoid the trap of building rapport with one person by

cutting down others. "When people bitch about or put down others,"Margaret says, "I have to wonder what they're going to say about me." Speak pleasantly and positively, and people will have pleasant and positive associations with you.

8. If you like a person, say so specifically. A genuine tactful compliment is a great way to solidify rapport. Make sure the compliment is specific and nonthreatening (that is, it is not suggestive or prematurely intimate). Some good compliments include: "I enjoy talking to you because you know how to listen." "I admire anyone who is as self-motivated as you are." "The colors you wear bring out the best in you." "You really know how to turn a funny phrase." "I find your smile absolutely infectious." And so on.

9. Above all, relax, smile and enjoy yourself! Being relaxed is contagious. When people are trying too hard, they are obviously not relaxed. And that makes others nervous as well. If you find conversation a trying experience, stop trying. Go for some fun activity, and invite the other person along.

KEY 29

"To turn contacts into friends, you must be able to move away from what you don't want, toward what you do."

There are times when you will meet someone and rapport will be so instant and powerful that you end up spending the entire evening with that individual and ignoring everyone else. But that is a relatively rare occurrence. Most people, even those we like right away, take some time to grow on us. In the context of a social event, this usually means ending the conversation—at least temporarily—and moving on to other people and activities. So the question is, how do you end a conversation and let the other person know that you are—or are not—interested in further contact? Let's first suppose you are not interested. How do you bow out politely?

Fortunately, there are a number of ways to exit gracefully. Most conversations have a natural end. If you want to move on during this lull, simply smile, thank the person, and leave. If there's an activity you are ready to resume, this provides a good opportunity to exit and move on. Otherwise, you can feel free to say you are going off to the restroom or to get some punch or to talk to some other friends or just to circulate. This is social party behavior, and the other person will generally smile and respond in kind. You might also say you enjoyed the conversation (if you did) and you would like to continue the conversation later (if you mean it).

Even if you like the other person, it's sometimes a good idea to have a "time out" so that you both can reflect on the experience. Many of the people we spoke with reported meeting someone they liked, then drifting away and coming back together throughout the evening. Says Margaret, "After I met this man I really liked and talked with him for about an hour, I felt fine about our going our own ways for a while. I guess it was because I felt confident that we had created some rapport." If you have created rapport and told the other person you enjoyed the conversation, that should be enough to establish a positive contact. Make it a point to talk with that person again later in the evening.

But suppose this is someone you're not that interested in and he or she won't take the hint. Then what? How do you continue to be polite—and also firmly let the other person know that you are moving on? The first and easiest thing to do is wind down the conversation and extend the physical distance between you. If that doesn't work, simply excuse yourself and move to another group or activity. There are various other techniques you can try, depending upon your personality and mood. If you find yourself set upon by a "glom," you might mention your boyfriend, your girlfriend, or your twelve kids. Or you might take the other person by the hand and introduce him or her to someone else. At a seminar, Jim was invited to lunch by a woman he didn't want to spend the entire lunch time talking with. Thinking quickly, he told her, "There's a group of us going out, and you're welcome to join us if you'd like." He then went and gathered a dozen or so people to be this "group."

Whatever you do, don't let your desire to be polite interfere with moving towards what you do want, and away from what you don't. You have every right to talk with—or not talk with—anyone you please. If you find someone infringing on this right, set him straight—pronto. Strangers need to earn your respect and trust, and earn the right to become friends. If you feel you are being pressured or mistreated, or if the other person refuses to take the hint that you don't like the way things are going, excuse yourself immediately.

GRACEFUL EXITS

A compliment—if you mean it

A future invitation—if you mean it

A smile and a handshake

Introduce the person to other people, or include him in a larger group

Politely excuse yourself to see other friends or circulate

Thank the other person for the conversation

LESS-THAN-GRACEFUL EXITS

Anything that can be construed as a put-down

Rudeness, crudeness

Simply walking away and disappearing

Telling people you want to see them again when you don't

EXTENDING INVITATIONS

Now let's assume you like the other person and you would like to see him again. How do you extend an invitation in such a way that it makes it easy for him to say yes without feeling pressured? And how can you tell if the other person is interested even before you ask? Jim, one of the people we spoke with, says, "If I'm interested in someone, I will make a statement like, 'I really enjoyed talking with you' and then watch for the response. If I can see this person really light up and agree that our conversation was fun, I feel pretty safe in suggesting a future meeting. But if the person seems only lukewarm, I'm likely to be more cautious with my invitation."

Jim's suggestion is important for a number of reasons. First, it allows you to gauge her interest. If you tell her how much you enjoyed talking to her and it doesn't register more than a mild tremor on the Richter Scale of passion, you'll know the earth hasn't moved for her. You might decide to extend an invitation anyway, to a party or other group event. That way, you can get to know the person—and have her get to know you—over a period of time. Keep in mind that first meetings are not always the best. A number of people told us of times they met someone and were not initially excited or even interested. Yet after a while they warmed up to this person, and a few people even reported meeting their spouses in this way. There's no need to be in a hurry. Remember, you can build a friendship one look, one conversation, one meeting at a time. Take all the time you need.

TIPS FOR EXTENDING INVITATIONS

1. Mention an activity or event you know they will attend. This is the easiest invitation to extend, and it's a way to show interest in future contact. Examples: "I'll see you in class next week." "I'll see you at the next meeting." "Are you going to the picnic on Sunday?" If it feels right, you might ask if he wants to share a ride or meet beforehand. Or you may find that he asks you.

2. If you uncovered any mutual interests in the course of your conversation, suggest doing one of those activities at some future time. Says Jeff: "I was talking with a woman I really liked, and I was wondering how I was going to ask her out. At one point, the conversation shifted to jazz and she said she loved to check out new jazz clubs. That was the chance I was looking for. I told her that a new club opened in town and asked if she wanted to check it out together. She said she did, and we set up a time."

3. If you've discovered some common interests, but don't feel comfortable asking for an actual date, suggest a group activity. (For example, "A group of us play volleyball on Tuesday nights. Why don't you join us next week?" or "The bicycle touring club has a ride every Sunday morning. Why don't you come with us this Sunday?" or "Some friends and I are going to the big chili cook-out next weekend. Want to come with us?") If he seems enthusiastic, you might suggest going together or getting together afterward. But remember, there's no need to rush things.

4. Make the invitation as nonthreatening as possible. Anything with a natural time limit on it—like lunch or coffee or a drink after work—is safer than asking for a Saturday night date. A date may be too big a decision—and you may get turned down. It is a common pattern for people to ask for too much too soon and then assume they've been rejected when the other person says no. If even a lunch date seems like too big a leap, suggest a get-together with other people. Here you have the option of going together or separately. And don't forget to include some mutually enjoyable activity in your plans.

5. Always be specific about any invitations. Avoid questions like "What are you doing Saturday night?" Suggest specific events at specific times. " 'We should get together sometime,' " Cindy says, "seems to be a polite way of saying nothing." Women we spoke with told us they were turned off by guys who ask for their number and then don't call. If you're not interested, don't ask. And don't accept.

6. Invite the person to leave when you leave. Going out somewhere and continuing the conversation over a snack is particularly appealing because sharing food is an excellent way to build rapport. Here, it's best if you have established definite rapport and the other person is moving at a similar pace. Certainly this is less threatening when there are others involved (i.e., "A group of us are going to get dessert downtown. Would you like to join us?").

7. If you feel uncomfortable inviting people out, use this discomfort to your advantage. For example, some women feel uncomfortable asking men out because they're afraid they'll be thought too forward. You can check this out beforehand, in the course of the conversation. Find a way to ask, "Do you like it when women ask you out?" Another technique is to admit feeling uncomfortable but to ask anyway. Vulnerability can be a great bridge-builder. On the other hand, no need to be a wimp.

8. If asking for someone's phone number for the specific reason of going out is too big a step, find another reason. Some non-threatening approaches include: "I'm having a party in a couple of weeks and I'd like to invite you. How can I get hold of you?" "Remember that book you said you'd be interested in seeing? I can't remember the author, but if you call me I'm sure I can find it." "Should I put you on the mailing list for our next bicycle trek?" "I have that information on the Ernie Kovacs video at home. Can I give you a call?"

9. Be sure and refer to some shared fun activity and mutual interest. Suppose the person you are interested in is leaving and you don't feel comfortable asking specifically for future contact. Then what? When you notice the person is about to leave, make it a point of saying goodbye and telling her you enjoyed spending time with her. Says Judy, "I met a guy I liked but I just couldn't bring myself to ask him out. When I noticed he was leaving, I walked over and told him I enjoyed meeting him. That apparently was enough of an invitation. He ended up asking me out." If the person doesn't respond that way (particularly if he or she seems too shy to offer an invitation), you might offer to exchange business cards or phone numbers. Remember, you—and everyone else—has every right to decline requests for business cards, phone numbers, or other private information. If you have no business cards or the phone number seems like too big a request, you can ask: "Just how do you spell your last name?" "Are you in the phone book, and would you like me to call you sometime?" "Can I reach you at work?"

What if the person in question has already left, or you feel uncomfortable about even asking his last name? You might first go to a mutual friend to find out if the person is available, and whether he might welcome an unsolicited phone call. Or, if you know his last name or place of work you might do a little sleuth work and give him a call. How will the call be received? You can't really know. The person might be pleasantly surprised, flattered even. Or he might feel as if his privacy has been invaded. If the latter is the case, all you can do is apologize and not take up much of his time. It seems as if the benefits here outweigh the risks. At the risk of appearing foolish or being turned down (by someone you hardly know!), you stand to gain a new friend.

10. If you are reluctant to call someone on the phone, the mail might work for you. Laura recalls meeting a man at an antique show and enjoying his company. "He seemed a little shy," she says, "but definitely interested. So I sent him an invitation to a party I was having, and I was sure to mention our mutual interest in antiques. I was delighted when he came, and we ended up going out for quite a while." Beware of sending a note that is too intimate, however, or else you'll risk scaring the person off. Keep the tone friendly, low-key, and fun.

11. Keep in mind that one of the purposes in meeting people is cultivating a social activities network. Therefore, don't disqualify people from future contact just because you don't see them as potential dating partners! A recent article in *Psychology Today* revealed that more than ever before, single Americans are cultivating opposite-sex friendships. We're convinced that friendship is the necessary foundation for any romantic relationship. Even if there's no romantic spark, if you like and enjoy being with certain people, go for future contact. Remember that if you like them and enjoy similar activities, you will probably like their friends as well.

12. Finally, relax and enjoy yourself. Just as you make contact and establish rapport with others most easily when you're having a great time, the best time to extend an invitation is when you're flushed with the excitement of fun. One of the women we interviewed told of a time she and a friend were at a restaurant. They were laughing and joking and telling stories, and she noticed a man who kept looking at her. In the excitement of the conversation, her friend persuaded her to write the man a witty note and have the waitress give it to him. She did, and the man later called. "It was something I never would have done," she admitted, "but we were just so high from laughing, I figured it was worth the risk."

FUTURE CONTACT STARTERS
A relaxed, playful attitude
Clearly letting the other person know you're interested
Creative invitations
Giving the other person space to accept or decline
Letting the other person know you had fun
Making the invitation as nonthreatening as possible
Suggesting definite activities at definite times
Suggesting mutually enjoyable activities

FUTURE CONTACT STOPPERS
Asking for too much too soon
Automatically assuming the person is interested
Being vague or evasive about your interest in the other person
Inability to take no for an answer
Insincerity
Obvious ploys for bed
Vague suggestions

DECLINING INVITATIONS

Just as sure as you're going to be asking for future contact, you are going to have an opportunity to say no as well. One of the biggest barriers to saying no is our well-intentioned desire not to hurt anyone's feelings. Many people never get started meeting people because they don't feel comfortable turning down an invitation or saying goodbye. That was particularly true of a number of the women we spoke with. Says Margaret, "It makes me angry at myself when I think of how many invitations to parties I turned down just because I figured there'd be guys there I'd have to turn down. So to avoid the hassle, I avoided a lot of situations." Ironically, it was a persistent caller who helped Margaret turn around her reluctance to say no. "There was this guy who I had gone out with years ago who was back in town. I went out with him once and realized we had little in common. But he kept calling me—every week. I had to keep saying no over and over again. After a while, I realized that I was no longer avoiding situations where I would have to turn invitations down." Surprisingly, men also have trouble turning down invitations. Says Jim, "It's sort of a new thing for women to be direct about wanting to get together. It isn't easy to say no gracefully." Women have known that for years. So how do you turn someone down without turning them off?

First of all, distinguish between saying no to the activity and saying no to the person. If this is someone you are interested in spending time with, but the activity is inappropriate, suggest something else ("No I don't think I want to go skydiving this weekend, but I wouldn't mind going to a movie"). If the time isn't right, suggest another time ("I already have plans for Monday, but I'm free Tuesday and Friday evening"). As difficult as it is to say no directly, don't extend the possibility of a future meeting if you have no intention to go out with this person. It just isn't fair to them. No matter how disappointing it is to be turned down, just about everyone we spoke with said they preferred a direct no to wasting time with someone who was "trying to be nice."

If you like the person but aren't looking for a dating partner, say so. Consider inviting that person to get-togethers to meet your friends, and suggest the same to them. It is perfectly acceptable to tell someone you like them, but are not interested in dating or are otherwise involved. If they don't take the hint, follow the same procedure for ending an unpleasant conversation. State in no uncertain terms that you are not interested, and put physical distance between yourself and this other person. If you and this person have mutual friends, you might consider relaying this information through a friend. If at all possible, avoid putting the other person down. Offer to stay on friendly terms, but make sure these are YOUR terms.

You now have a pretty good idea of how YOU can best meet the people you want to meet. But there's still a piece missing. How do you turn contacts into friendship, and how do you develop these budding friendships in a way that benefits you and the other person? How do you find out whether there's a match in Life Stage, Life Course, Life-style, and other aspects of your social agendas? In the next chapter, we will discuss building the foundation for the friendships and relationships you want in your life.

Chapter 13

"Turning acquaintances into friends"

The other evening you were at a get-together where there were both friends and people you didn't know. In the middle of a conversation about a great time you had, you suddenly found yourself talking to a new person. Several times in the course of the evening you reconnected, and when it was time to go home, you both decided you wanted to get together again and exchanged phone numbers.

Now, it's three days later and you still feel a tingle of excitement when you think about this person. You also feel a little bit of apprehension when you think about getting to know someone new. Your thoughts drift to all of those great expectations you had in the past—that turned to disappointment. Like that really promising guy you met a year ago who forgot to tell you he was married until you were already deeply involved. Or the woman who wore high heels on your wilderness camping trip, and forever dashed your hopes of turning her into an outdoorswoman. Then you remember those very special relationships in your life, the one or two that worked for a long period of time, and you wonder, "Will this new acquaintance that I like so much right now turn into a really important person in my life?" Yes, there seems to be chemistry. But you're wise enough to know that it's a long way from the spark of chemistry to the steady warmth of friendship.

As you ponder how you will get to know this new person, many questions fill your mind: How do I know if I can trust this person with my feelings, aspirations, doubts, secrets? How can I find out if we're really compatible? Will we genuinely like each other? And if we do get close, how do I keep from losing myself in the relationship?

This chapter is about turning acquaintances into friends. Fortunately, the same process you used to meet new people can be used to make friends. Shared activity, shared social agenda, shared social networks, shared preparation, shared communication—all will help you become closer to your new friend and decide what part you will play in each others' lives. Remember, not everyone is destined to be your life partner, nor will everyone you meet or like become a close friend. However, the people you do meet and like— even if they turn out to be only casual friends—can introduce you to the social activities networks where you MAY meet the people you will know for the rest of your life. If you keep this simple fact in mind, you won't be hampered by disappointment when things don't work out, and you'll keep moving steadily toward bringing the kinds of people you like into your life.

KEY 30

"Fun kindles the spark of chemistry into the warmth of friendship."

"I remember when my husband and I took our first trip together," recalls Kathy. "It was nearly fifteen years ago, and we went to a bluegrass festival where we had a terrific time. It was a warm day in June, and we were in the convertible with the top down, the wind blowing my hair all over the place. I remember we were listening to tapes of the music we'd heard at the festival, and to this day I get a special feeling when I hear certain songs. We were just getting to know each other in those days and we talked all the way back about our plans for our lives, and all the other interests we shared."

Jerry has this to say about Tony, his lifelong friend: "When we were teenagers back in Chicago, we used to spend our Saturdays walking all over the city. We'd start out after breakfast and sometimes we didn't get back until dinner time. We'd talk about the girls we liked, our career aspirations, the White Sox, the world situation—anything and everything. We never ran out of things to do or say. But most of all, we loved baseball. I remember the year the White Sox won the pennant, Tony and I went to at least a dozen games. We never went with anyone else, and we'd replay the games over and over on the way home. Then all winter he'd come over and we'd play baseball board games. And we were always laughing. Even though we only see each other a few times a year, we're still very, very close. And it's a funny thing, but to this day I can't think about baseball and not think of Tony."

If you stop to think about it, it's the shared activity and fun you think about when you think of your closest friends. Sure, you've shared some sad moments, some harsh words. Your friend or mate has supported you through difficult times, and you've done the same in return. But when you come right down to it, it's the fun you remember. Because if it wasn't fun being with this person, you wouldn't have chosen to be around them. So it is with new acquaintances. If you want to turn these into friendship, first see if the fun is there.

How do you decide what activities to do with a new acquaintance? Choose something that's fun for you and that you think might be fun for the other person. And choose an activity that will help you get to know the new person. And be sure to listen carefully enough so that you know if this activity is right for your new acquaintance. Stop for a moment now and think about how YOU best get to know new people. Is it through sports? A shared experience, like a concert or movie? Conversation? Dinner? A long walk? A vigorous activity like dancing or racquetball?

Since Bill is an outdoorsy kind of person, he likes to get to know new acquaintances through camping. "That's where I really come alive," he says. "I'm in my element. I love to share the quiet and the magic of the woods with a new friend. Since my life is about being outdoors, suggesting an outing outdoors—even just a hike—

lets me know whether this woman I like is really for me. A hike always builds rapport," he says, "or lets me know she's not my type."

Grace, who's the athletic type, likes to invite her new acquaintances to play volleyball. "It's not that the guy has to be some kind of super jock," she says. "But I find I really learn a lot about people from the way they play the game. I like someone who plays the game intensely but has fun. The things I notice are, does he go for it? Is he a team player? Does he hog the ball, or is he sensitive to letting everyone participate? I also like to invite women friends to play volleyball. Since I'm fairly active, I relate best to women who can hold their own in competition. I get irritated when women just stand there and let the ball drop or allow themselves to be intimidated by the men players."

Joyce prefers everyday activities—like walking her dog or having breakfast. "I love to walk, and I love to walk my dog. And I find this can tell me a lot about the men I go out with. I know a lot of people in town, and I often run into them in the park or downtown. It's always interesting to see my date's response when I stop and talk with people I know. Sometimes he'll get right into the swing of things, and that's a good sign because it means he enjoys people as much as I do. But if the guy is put off by my familiarity with people, then it's an indication he's not for me. Another thing I love is long, leisurely breakfasts. Some of my best times have been relaxing on a Sunday morning, just doing nothing. If my new friend can't sit still even for a moment, then I know he's not someone I can relax with."

Like Joyce, Hank finds a good conversation over a great meal an excellent way to get to know a new acquaintance. "I have this favorite restaurant that I like to go to with old friends and new friends alike. First of all, it's the kind of food I love. Secondly, I have so many positive memories that I automatically glow whenever I go there. Of course, I always make sure the other person enjoys that kind of food; if not, we go somewhere else. But the main thing is, I love good conversation. Sitting and enjoying great food and conversation is a way for me to feel really close to a new friend."

Charles told us he became close to a new woman friend through music. "Janis told me she played flute, so I brought my guitar over there one Saturday afternoon. After about three minutes, it felt like we'd been playing together forever. It was a lot like a conversation and a lot like a dance. After playing music for two hours, I felt I knew Janis better than if we'd talked for two days straight."

Other people told us they get to know new people through dancing, playing cards, going to movies and discussing them, concerts, even doing errands. "It's funny," says Jane, "how errands and mundane chores can be so much more fun with another person. One of the first dates I had with the man I'm seeing now involved getting our résumés printed and mailed. We were so busy talking, I didn't even mind being stuck in traffic! We had some time left over, so we did some shopping and he ended up treating me to ice cream. It was one of the most enjoyable afternoons I've spent in a long time!"

Turn to the list of enjoyable activities in Chapter Three (or your own list) and notice which ones you have used in the past to get to know new people. What have these experiences told you about your new acquaintance? What is it about these activities that is so revealing? Now make your own new list: ACTIVITIES THAT HELP ME GET TO KNOW PEOPLE.

You may find the activities on your list are varied, or that they fall into a particular pattern. For example, some people find they get to know people best through physical activity. This can include sports, indoor fix-it work, gardening, or hiking. Some people like people-oriented affairs like parties, dances, personal growth workshops, while others prefer more intimate activity—quiet conversation, long walks, a dinner. Some people prefer the visual, such as movies and art museums, while others like to listen to concerts. Some enjoy creative activities such as sketching or playing music together. Among those who enjoy conversation, there are those who like to talk about people, those who would rather talk about things, those who love ideas, and those who prefer talking about activities. As you look at your list of ACTIVITIES THAT HELP ME GET TO KNOW PEOPLE, note the following:

What kinds of activity do I prefer for having fun and getting to know people?

1. Physically active
2. People-oriented
3. Intimate
4. Shared visual or auditory experience
5. Creative

What kinds of conversations do I prefer for getting to know new acquaintances?

1. About ourselves (our mutual interests, our feelings, our aspirations)
2. About others (psychology, people we know or observe, celebrities)

3. About things (new cars, places to eat, clothes)
4. About ideas (philosophy, religion, books, science, politics)
5. About activities (sports, fun ski weekends, travel)

Once you've answered these questions, you have a pretty good idea of what you like to do to get to know people. But you still don't know how that will work with your new acquaintances. Knowing what YOU like to do will help you create a "menu" for them to choose from when you extend an invitation of your own or respond to suggestions of theirs. Be sure you include a variety of activities on your menu, and be sure you find out which activities will help others get to know you.

KEY 31

"Open-ended invitations are a perfect way to find out what the other person enjoys."

It's Tuesday evening at 9:00 and David is nervously pacing back and forth between his kitchen and living room. At least three times he reaches for the phone—but thinks better of it and goes to the refrigerator for a snack instead. "This is ridiculous," David says to himself. "If I don't call her soon, I'm gonna get so fat she won't even recognize me." He thinks back to the previous Thursday evening when he met Lynn at a film writing class. They seemed to hit it off well, and at the end of the evening they agreed to "get together sometime" and exchanged phone numbers.

It's now 9:15 and David is rehearsing all kinds of unpleasant scenarios in his head: Suppose a man answers? What if she laughs? Or says, "Who? I don't know anyone named David"? And even if she seems glad to talk with me, how will I invite her out? And what will I invite her to? Maybe she'll call me first, he thinks to himself. Nah, he couldn't count on that. Besides, he'd recently read an article that said that the longer you wait to get together with a new acquaintance, the less likely you are to do it. He remembers a number of people he had met, liked, and promised to call—but never did. Spurred by those memories, he grasps the phone with quivering hand and begins dialing . . .

While David is dialing Lynn's number, let's consider his

options. First of all, he can simply start a conversation and eventually get around to asking her if she'd like to do something sometime. Or he can begin right away with a request for Lynn to join him for a specific activity at a specific place and a specific time. Those are the two extremes. The first we call an "open-ended invitation," the second a "closed invitation." Which is likely to work best? That depends on the people, and it depends on the situation. Closed invitations are particularly appropriate in business situations where you have a limited time frame and a specific objective. People commonly receive business calls that immediately ask for an appointment. In the context of business, they aren't usually put off by it.

But in getting to know a new acquaintance, it's usually not a good idea to begin the conversation immediately with a very specific "closed" invitation. First of all, you have no idea what state of mind the person is in when you call. Let's say she was doing her taxes, writing a long letter to an old friend, or watching her favorite show on TV (and she hates being interrupted). It's going to take some time to change gears and get used to having you on the phone. And it's going to take you some time to get a feeling for her mood and what kind of activity she's likely to be interested in. Let's check back with David and see how his phone call to Lynn is going . . .

LYNN: *Hello.*

DAVID: *Hi, Lynn, this is David. We met at the film class—*

LYNN: *Sure. Good to talk to you again. What's up?*

DAVID: *Is this a good time to talk for a bit?*

LYNN: *Oh, yeah. I'm just winding down from a day at work, and I was going to work on that script treatment.*

DAVID: *I remember you telling me the other evening about how you were doing a children's film on gardening. How's that coming?*

Notice what David did. He prevented embarrassment by identifying himself right away and put himself "in context." Lynn knew immediately who he was, and she appreciated his telephone manners, particularly when he asked if she were available to talk. He then picked up on her response and used it to bring her back to the enjoyable conversation they had had about a mutual interest a few days earlier. That is a very important step. One of the ways you can re-establish rapport with a new acquaintance is to refer to an enjoyable experience you shared. Now let's look at some alternative scenarios.

What if Lynn didn't remember him? Even if she didn't know who he was immediately, David could have brought the conversation back to their fun time the previous week, and possibly added a gentle joke. Actually, something similar happened to a woman we spoke with. She had gone out on a blind date with a somewhat shy but otherwise delightful man, then boldly called to ask him over for dinner. To her—and his—embarrassment, he didn't remember her name and seemed very distant over the phone. She hung up, vowing never again to ever, ever call a man.

A few weeks later, she ran into him in another setting and he apologized. It seemed that he was so surprised to hear from her that he had no idea who she was. Because he was so embarrassed, he felt more and more like crawling into the woodwork. Fortunately, our friend was able to resurrect rapport, and the two later ended up marrying.

Another possibility is that your phone call is ill-timed. Always ask permission to talk, and always find out if the timing is right. If your new friend says, "Actually, this ISN'T a good time . . ." find out what would be a better time. A quick word here about two dubious advances in communications technology: "call waiting" and the telephone answering machine. "Call waiting" is a setup whereby you can tell if someone else is trying to call you while you are on the phone. This generally means excusing yourself from party A to find out who party B is and what he or she wants. As useful as this setup can be in the business setting, it can be very exasperating socially. So don't be surprised if the person you are speaking to hastily asks permission to call you back because she's on the line with someone else. If you BOTH have call waiting, this can add to the frustration—but also to the humor and rapport.

What if you call and get someone's telephone answering machine? If it's someone you know well who could easily call you back, you probably wouldn't hesitate to leave a message. But a very new acquaintance might hesitate to call you back. What if you leave a message and he/she doesn't call? And what if you don't leave a message? A friend reports that a woman friend of his reached him after many phone calls and said, "I've been trying to reach you for WEEKS!" This surprised him, because she hadn't left a message on his answering machine. But she just didn't feel comfortable doing it. Some people are like that.

Our suggestion is, if you feel comfortable leaving a light, playful message, do that. If you don't want the other person to feel obligated to return your call, say you'll call back, and leave them with a little joke or reminder of your good time together. Another friend of ours loves to sing his own version of "Strangers in the Night" into people's answering machines, changing the words to "strangers in the night, exchanging messages, wondering in the night just what the message is . . ."

But what about David and Lynn? They're engrossed in conversation, and now they've warmed up sufficiently for David to get to the point of the call:

DAVID: *... You remember that list of ten things we're supposed to notice about the films we see? I was thinking about trying that out at a movie this weekend, and I was wondering if you wanted to go with me.*

LYNN: *Sounds like a great idea. What do you want to see?*

DAVID: *I remember you saying that you like films from the Forties, and I notice* The Best Years of Our Lives *is playing on campus Friday evening at 9:30.*

LYNN: *No kidding? I've never seen that one, but I've always wanted to.*

DAVID: *Great. Since the film doesn't start until 9:30, would you like to have some dinner first?*

Lynn seems excited about going to the movie with David, and the conversation turns to restaurants. They both rule out "Wok Around The Clock," an all-night Chinese restaurant as "too noisy," and "Miss Steak" as overrated and overpriced, and settle on a romantic Spanish restaurant a few blocks from the theater. Then they confirm the time and place, say their goodbyes and hang up.

Notice that David presented his idea as just an option, and he geared it toward something he knew Lynn was already interested in. He wanted to make sure that the specific invitation he offered was one she was likely to accept. In making a decision about where to go to eat, David made sure that Lynn had ample opportunity to voice her choice. He also stated his own preference, and this set up the framework for any future invitations. Both would offer suggestions, and the final decision would be arrived at together. In the dance of getting to know one another, they now knew that each would have a turn to lead. Not every couple or group of friends likes it that way, but Lynn and David do, and we have found that when relationships are balanced in this respect, people are more likely to develop communication and respect in other areas of the relationship.

Of course, telephone conversations can also raise serious

questions about new acquaintances. Marjorie reports: "I met a guy I liked at a dance and he asked for my phone number. He called, and after we talked for a while, he told me he was in the Navy. That turned me off to going out with him because I'm not all that fond of military life. I'm looking for a serious partner right now, and I just can't see myself traveling around the world trying to raise a family or else waiting patiently while my man is away for four months. I told him very politely that there was nothing wrong with him, but that I didn't have the time and energy to start anything that couldn't go anywhere."

KEY 32

"If you want to kindle a flame, look for a match."

As you extend invitations to new acquaintances, be sure to choose activities that are likely to reveal whether that person is a good match for you, not only in terms of shared interests but also in personality traits, values, and life-style. Do you learn about other people through conversation? Sports? Working together? Playing together? Dancing? Listening to concerts? Watching a movie? Playing board games? Just going for a long walk? Find out how the other person enjoys getting to know a new person, and mutually decide on an activity that will allow that person to learn who you are as well. It's essential that you know what you want and what you don't want in a new friend or relationship. That way, you will have some way of deciding whether you want to continue getting to know this new person—or if you want to put on the brakes.

Todd reports that he asked a new acquaintance to accompany him to the hospital where he had volunteered to bring gifts and entertain shut-ins at Christmas time. "I had a sense she would enjoy the activity," Todd says, "and I was right. I really liked the way she got right into the swing of things, and enjoyed the people and the activity as much as I did. I realized that not everyone could appreciate that kind of 'date,' and that was the beginning of us becoming much closer."

For Cheryl, however, a jazz concert pointed out some serious differences between her and her date. "I loved the concert," she says, "and he hated it. Said it was too loud for him. That seemingly unimportant incident pointed out some differences that were reflected in other areas of our relationship. I realized that he tended to be much more subdued and laid back, while I was more high-energy, outgoing, and active. Things sort of fizzled between us after that evening."

When you first begin spending time with a new acquaintance, there's a tendency to smooth over and minimize differences. After all, if you didn't like the person, you wouldn't be spending time with him in the first place. Why not give him the benefit of the doubt? But just as you look for ways you match, be aware of mismatches as well. Of course it's disappointing when you like someone and it doesn't work out. But it's important to see it as a mismatch, not a rejection, and remember that the sea is more abundant with fish than you think.

What traits, values, and interests do you consider most important in a friend or lover? Which traits and values would immediately turn you off to someone? Look back to the lists you made in Chapter Four of the people you've liked most and what you enjoyed about them. Also look at the list of people you have liked, enjoyed, and admired least. Now be even more specific about the traits you like and dislike. We have listed below some of the traits people told us made them want to get to know a new acquaintance—and some of the ones that caused them to turn off. This list is just to "prime the pump" and indicate the vast differences between human beings. Choose only those "go-ers" and "stoppers" that are most important to you.

MENU OF GO-ERS

Able to make long-term friends

Adventurous

Allow me to be open

Balanced between talking, listening

Bring out the joy in me

Easygoing

Enjoy what they do

Enthusiastic

Follow up

Good conversationalists

Have a sense of humor

Have good manners

Have similar interests and beliefs

Honest

Intelligent

Know how to have fun

Listen well

Look for the good

Nonphony	Thoughtful
Playful	Touch appropriately
Reveal themselves	Trusting and trustworthy
Receptive	Uninhibited
Show self-confidence	Warm
Sincerely compliment	

MENU OF STOPPERS

Abusive or inconsiderate	Interrupt
Become too intimate too soon	Judgmental, critical of others
Blaming	Mind-reading
Come on too strong	Not perceptive
Complain	Possessive
Don't know what they like	Self-centered
Don't know how to listen	Too changeable
"Dump" feelings on you	Too confrontive on values
Have bad manners	Treat others badly
Have old-fashioned attitudes about women	Try too hard
Hold in feelings	Unable to keep friends
Hostile	Unresponsive

As you will probably notice from the list of stoppers, one of the prime turn-offs has to do with coming on too strong rather than respecting the other person's rate and pace. So, during this first phase, go slowly and take the time to find out about the other person and let that person get to know you. Margaret told us that when she was in her early twenties, it was fashionable and acceptable to sleep with someone almost immediately. "I remember several times," she says, "when I fell in love at first sight, but because I didn't see past the first sight, I didn't really know the person I was getting involved with. I would end up attempting to justify having slept with this person—and ignoring his more negative traits.

"Now," she says, "my attitude is go more slowly and find out if we LIKE each other. Going slowly gives me a chance to step back and really notice what I want in a person. It lets me see the good parts, the bad parts, the total person I'm getting involved with. And I can ask myself, 'Can I work with these traits?' I respect a guy who will hang in there and get to know me first and create a solid base for a relationship. Intimacy has to be a natural result of getting to know someone over time."

We couldn't agree more. Move slowly, and you are likely to avoid regret. Or as one of the people we spoke with said, "Better a small disappointment up front than a huge one down the road."

YOUR ACTION PLAN FOR
TURNING ACQUAINTANCES INTO FRIENDS

1. Make a list of *Activities that Help Me Know People,* and choose those activities that will help you get to know a new acquaintance, and let the person know you.

2. When extending invitations to others, use shared activities and previous fun as a bridge. Be sure you begin with open-ended invitations, and give your partner an opportunity to help decide on the activity.

3. Be sure you are moving at a pace slow enough to get to know a person over time. Avoid the trap of too close, too soon.

4. Remember, even if a person doesn't become a close friend or life partner, if you like him you will probably like his social activities networks as well.

Chapter 14

"Where do you want your new friend to fit in your life?"

The bonds of friendship and intimacy are among the greatest rewards in life. As with other kinds of "bonds," if we invest wisely we can reap lifelong dividends. Since we do not have the time and energy to invest in everyone we meet, we must choose carefully.

Obviously, not everyone is suited to be a mate, a best friend, or even a friend. Just because you enjoy bowling with someone doesn't mean you want to have six kids with him. The partner you are so close with at work may share none of your leisure interests and few of your values. And even your favorite dating partner might not be someone you could live with. The process of getting to know people involves deciding how and where you want them to fit into your life—and respecting their decisions about how they want you to fit into theirs.

Choosing a bowling partner is a pretty straightforward procedure: Can he bowl? Does he enjoy it? Is he likely to show up? Does he have a good disposition? Does he fit in with the rest of the team? Choosing a life partner is a bit more complicated, and a bit more serious. Besides enjoying similar activities, genuinely liking each other, and having a certain chemistry between you, there are three very important things to consider in choosing a mate or life partner: Life Stage, Life Course, and Life-Style. In Chapter Four, you used these as a way of determining your social agenda. Now let's look at how these factors come into play when choosing a long-term partner.

LIFE STAGE   The first time Tracy and Bill met, there was an instant attraction. They immediately began going out, and became very close in a short period of time. It didn't seem to matter at first that there was a ten-year difference in their ages. After they had been going together for a few months, however, they ran into a serious problem. Bill, who was in his early thirties, wanted to get married and have a family. Tracy, who had just graduated from college, was reluctant to make a commitment of any kind. She wasn't sure of her career goals, and wanted to travel. She saw herself having kids, but not until she was thirty or so. They were at an impasse. They went though a series of angry break-ups and reconciliations, with Bill accusing Tracy of being "irresponsible" and Tracy calling Bill "oppressive." They finally ended up going their separate ways—on good terms—once they realized that they had irreconcilable differences in Life Stage. Bill was ready to settle down, and Tracy was not. Their positions weren't good or bad, right or wrong—just different.

What is your Life Stage right now? What are you looking for? A series of casual dating partners? Marriage? A family? As you get to know someone you are considering as a life partner (or for that matter, someone who is looking at you in that way), notice if there's a match in Life Stage. If your Life Stages are different, that doesn't mean you cannot have a relationship. But it does make sense to communicate and negotiate those differences up front—rather than dealing with frustration and disappointment farther down the line.

LIFE-STYLE   Jeff loved to socialize. A musician, he enjoyed staying out late and partying. When he met Mary, he was attracted to her quiet dedication. Mary worked as a nurse, and Jeff admired the way she served other people. For Mary, Jeff was like a bright light who entered her life. Because they liked each other so much, they tried to accommodate each other at first. Mary would accompany Jeff to parties or music gigs, but never would get into the swing of things. So Jeff decided that Mary was important enough to him to give up music. This went on for over a year, until Jeff noticed himself becoming distant and resentful towards Mary. He realized he had been denying an important part of himself by giving up music. So he announced to Mary that he was going to play again. She interpreted this change as a betrayal—she had devoted herself to him with the unspoken understanding that he was giving up the musician's life. Although by that time they loved each other very much, Jeff and Mary were unable to resolve a basic Life-Style difference—and they broke up.

Life-Style consists of the things we like to do, and the way we enjoy doing them. Jeff thought he could change his Life-Style, but didn't realize how much music was a part of who he was. Jennifer, another person we spoke with, told us that a boyfriend broke up with her because he didn't like her hugging other people, men or women. For each of them, this was an important enough Life-Style issue to come between them. "If he had asked me to wear different clothes or to try a new activity," she says, "that would have been okay. But hugging is a part of me which I'm simply not willing to give up. It's nonnegotiable."

As you look at your style of living—the things you enjoy doing, your values, the people you like to be around—notice which are most important to you. Which are "nonnegotiable"? Religion? Your desire to travel? Having a family? Playing softball? Where you want to live? Going to bars? Monogamy? Your friends? Your career? Any one of these can become a potential pitfall if there is no match—and no negotiation.

LIFE COURSE Rich and Pam met when both were graduate students at a large university. They both loved movies, skiing, and even studied together. As students, they enjoyed commiserating about the student life-style and the courses they were taking. After a year together, they seriously discussed marriage. Both agreed that each person should have a career, and that child care should be shared. Upon graduation, they married and took jobs in their chosen fields, Rich in natural resources, Pam in business. Soon a basic—and touchy—conflict arose. Rich, who was dedicated to working to solve environmental problems, was earning less than Pam was in her job at a large corporation. Now that she was out of school, she had plenty of money to spend on clothes, travel, and expensive restaurants. Rich didn't. And what's more, it wasn't all that important to him. While Pam supported his ideals, she also wanted to live more elegantly than they could afford. In an effort to compromise, she suggested that Rich stay at his low-paying job for two years, then take a job in industry. He considered it, but then realized his interest in environmental issues wasn't a passing interest but a lifetime direction. Sadly, they went their separate ways.

Life Course has to do with your ultimate values, with your Life-Style over time. Life Course has to do with whether or not you want a family; whether you want to live in the city, the country, or the suburbs; your spiritual or religious principles; your ultimate purpose in life. Are you planning to be a "lifer" in the Navy? A professional athlete or entertainer? A member of the clergy? A poet? Are you determined to have enough kids to field a baseball team? Do you think it's important to live close to your parents? Do you want to be a world traveler? Are you dedicated to some political, social, or spiritual cause? Is it your life goal to become a billionaire? You'd better make sure than any long-term partner you choose can support—or at very least accept—these life goals.

Now let's consider your own Life Stage, Life-Style, Life Course and how they apply to the new people you've met by answering for yourself the following questions:

- As far as I can tell, what stage am I in now? What am I looking for? Am I ready for a new career, or perfectly happy in my present one? Ready to settle down, or just looking around? Am I up against the "biological clock" and ready to have kids? Am I willing to start a new family?
- What are the elements of my life-style? Which of these will I compromise on? Which are nonnegotiable?
- As far as I can see, what is my Life Course? Am I dedicated to any overriding purpose, principle, or goal? How is this likely to affect a long-term relationship? Which aspects of my Life Course am I willing to compromise on? Which are nonnegotiable?

Along with Life Stage, Life-Style, and Life Course, you will also want to determine your partner's criteria for a successful friendship or relationship. Ask yourself—and the other person—these questions: For you, what is important about friendship? About a primary relationship? And what will having that in your friendship or relationship do for you?

Remember, when it comes to Life Stage, Life-Style, Life Course, and what people desire in their personal relationships, there is no right or wrong—just matches and mismatches. Establish each of these as soon as you begin to get close to a person so that differences can be understood and if possible, ironed out. You can learn a lot about people just in the course of doing things together, but be sure and ask if there's any question as to their social agendas. Don't rely on assumptions or mind reading. Ask and communicate! Out of this you will create a mutual respect for differences that will result in a supportive friendship, even if you do not become life partners. Or, you may find yourself more willing to negotiate, or the other person more flexible than you thought. But consider any important differences a red flag that indicates something to be communicated and negotiated. Differences have a way of getting larger over time, particularly when they aren't communicated or resolved. Be aware of these pitfalls when getting to know someone new:

PITFALL 1. DELUSIONS OF "GLAND-EUR." Just because there is terrific chemistry between another person and yourself doesn't mean that you will be able to resolve all of your differences. When you allow your "glands" to speak without including your head in the process, you are building your relationship on hopes, expectations, and ultimately, fantasy. Keep in mind that chemistry can be more than physical attraction. There's a chemistry between good friends, and there's a chemistry that exists between long-term partners that has developed over time. "Glandular" chemistry is just the first step, and in itself does not insure successful relationships. Think about this: most marriages that later end up in divorce court begin with an ample amount of physical chemistry, but that chemistry fades when the other forms of chemistry fail to develop.

PITFALL 2. THE SCARCITY MODEL. It is unfortunately common for people to hold on to relationships that are not working because of a belief that they will never find anyone else. We don't recommend discarding people carelessly, but if you are stuck in a relationship because you're afraid there aren't enough potential partners out there, you've missed the point of this book. The best way to avoid fears of scarcity is to cultivate your social activities networks.

PITFALL 3. THE PERFECT MATE SYNDROME. Some people never find anyone because their standards are so high that God herself would flunk their test. These people will tend to consult a long list of attributes, but never really get to know anyone because they disqualify people too early. If this sounds familiar, go through your list of attributes and choose only those that are absolutely essential, and consider the rest luxuries. Leave your list at home UNTIL you've let other people tell you who THEY ARE instead of merely listening for what YOU WANT. One of the reasons people fall into the Perfect Mate Syndrome is to protect themselves against disappointing and unpleasant experiences. The same result can be accomplished by making sure you take all the time you need to get to know someone, and that you move at your own pace.

                PITFALL 4. THE MYTH OF REJECTION. We've said it before, we'll say it again—there is no such thing as rejection, only mismatches. Somewhere in your mind you've stored dozens of "rejection stories"—where either you are bitter because someone rejected you, or feel guilty about dumping someone else. Go through these stories right now, and notice how often rejection was really a difference in Life Stage, Life-Style, or Life Course. Do this anytime you are afraid of being rejected or rejecting someone else.

BLENDING: YOURS, MINE, AND OURS

                You've found a new friend you like more and more. You've shared some mutually enjoyable activities that have brought you closer. You have a realistic picture of where and how you would like this person to fit in your life, and you've decided to invest in the bonds of friendship. How do you insure getting closer and continuing to find out about one another? Once more—the foundation of friendship—and romance—is shared activities and enjoyable moments. But, you may be objecting, relationships are not all sweetness and light. Conflict is a part of every human relationship. You're right, but most relationships that don't make it die because the problems take over and the fun falls by the wayside. That's why it's important to establish a framework that insures you'll enjoy the time you spend together. That way, you will be motivated to handle the problems.

                We have found that the happiest and most satisfying relationships have included the following elements as a foundation: Communication, Mutuality, Sharing, and Fun and Adventure.

COMMUNICATION   As we've emphasized in this chapter, it's essential to let the other person know who you are and for you to find out about him or her. When you fail to communicate who you are up front, you create future difficulties. JoAnn had always been attracted to astrology and other forms of the occult. But when she met Greg, a successful attorney, she decided it wouldn't be appropriate to bring up that part of herself. After they had become a lot closer, they were watching a TV talk show where an astrologer was a guest. Greg began ranting and raving about astrology being akin to witchcraft, that it was crazy and irrational and he would never consort with anyone superstitious enough to believe in it. JoAnn didn't say anything, but she gradually withdrew from her relationship with Greg. She learned the sad lesson that it doesn't work to try to please or protect another person by withholding important parts of yourself.

On the other hand, when you let another person know who you are and pay attention to who that person is, you're both more likely to get what you want. Says Craig, "When I'm interested in someone, I like to listen for clues as to what she really wants and likes. Rita, the woman I'm going with, once mentioned that she wasn't allowed much creative freedom of expression when she was a child. So I've made it a point to appreciate that part of her now. And it's allowed us to become closer. It's also worked both ways. One time I was at her house and remarked how chilly it was. The next week, she had knitted me an afghan."

As you are developing rapport with a person, be sure to express your likes and dislikes—and respect the other person's. To avoid dwelling on dislikes only, use the "3 for 1" rule. For each thing you dislike that a person does, find three things you like. That way, you're investing in "bonds," not problems. Dislikes should be expressed in "I" rather than "you" statements. In other words, "I don't like it when you eat crackers in bed" is more useful and less threatening than "You drive me crazy when you eat crackers in bed!" The "I" statement suggests you are being responsible for your emotions rather than blaming the other person for what you feel.

Mary says, "It took me a long time to learn how to ask for things. I'd get very irritable and demanding, and when the other person didn't hop to it right away, I'd accuse him of not caring about me. Last summer, though, I tried staying with 'I' statements, and it really worked. My husband and I were vacationing, and I noticed I was starting to feel a little neglected. In the past, I would have said, 'You're not nurturing me.' This time I said, 'Jeff, I need some tender loving care.' I was amazed at how quickly he came over, put his arm around me, and just held me. He told me later that because I didn't demand it, he felt freer to give it."

An excellent way to improve communication is through—yes—shared fun activity. Helen reports that when she and her husband fight, a good antidote is to go out dancing. "We have so many wonderful memories of dancing," she says, "that we automatically fall into step with each other. Afterwards, we almost always come up with a solution to our problem."

MUTUALITY Bill knew his relationship with Amy was in trouble when the two of them signed up for jitterbug lessons. Although the dance was set up so that the man leads, Amy had a lot of trouble letting Bill lead. "To me," he said, "it pointed up the fact that we had a great deal of conflict over who was calling the shots in the relationship." When they first began going out, it was easy for the outgoing Bill to make all of the arrangements and set the tone. Amy, who was quieter by nature, seemed to go along with whatever was planned. After a while, though, Bill noticed that her acquiescence had turned to resentment. "I realized I should have consulted her on a lot of things earlier," Bill told us. "But since she didn't seem to mind, I never bothered to ask her what she wanted."

Like a smooth dance, a good relationship requires balance, harmony, cooperation, teamwork. Each person needs a chance to lead, and this pattern must be established from the very beginning. Make it a goal to identify what each person wants, and look for ways both people can be satisfied. By all means please the other person, but not if it means giving up an important part of yourself. The result will be blame and resentment when things don't work out. By all means respect yourself and the other person, and celebrate your similarities and differences.

SHARING Says Joan, "One of the first things my husband turned me on to when we met was meditation. It became a shared activity that we did together, something that I never would have done on my own. We still do it today." And Steve: "I came from a family where we never had anything on the walls, no decorations, pictures, or anything. So when I met Elizabeth, I was particularly attracted to how she made a living space look beautiful. We would go shopping together, and I think she's really taught me to appreciate beautiful things."

Other people we spoke with credited friends and lovers with introducing them to ice skating, love of travel, classical music, running, softball, even milking cows. Your close friends and partners are a doorway to an entirely new world of activities, ideas, ways of being. One of the most exciting things about being close to someone is sharing not only common interests, but the entire fabric of your life—work, family, friends, values. Bringing your entire life into a relationship allows you to build the relationship with the support of others—and make the relationship a part of your support system. As you grow closer to a special friend, you will want to share more and more of your life.

PLAY AND ADVENTURE Exploring life with a new person through shared activities can be as exciting as visiting a foreign land, sailing through uncharted waters, or climbing a mountain. The people we spoke with who developed lasting relationships look at those relationships as constant exploration, as adventures. They add enough play and novelty so that today's good times don't become tomorrow's ruts. "On Valentine's Day," Jackie says, "I brought my husband a six-pack with a card I took from a restaurant where we had a great time. It was great to see his face when he opened it, and I could tell he was remembering the great time we had. So he teased me and said he'd have to make me a candlelit dinner. Even though it was February, he grilled steaks on the barbecue. We had baked potatoes, wine, and he even found those stubby little candles for the table. The whole time during dinner, he told me all these nice things about myself and we spent the rest of the evening just talking about how lucky we were to be with each other."

Other people told us they kept the fires kindled by taking special trips, sending their mate surprise notes or gifts, thoughtful phone calls, secret dinners, or adventures with a few close friends. "I really enjoy surprising my girlfriend," Jim told us. "Life has its less pleasant surprises—so why not create some pleasant ones?"

ENDING OR CHANGING A RELATIONSHIP

The sad fact of life is that all relationships end, if not through disagreement, then through death. The emotional risk in getting close is knowing there WILL be an end and deciding to get close anyway. Many of us at some time in our lives hold back from intimacy because the loss would be too much to take—and yet our love of life and desire for intimacy eventually win out. We continue to take risks.

Sometimes differences in Life Stage, Life-Style, and Life Course are too much to reconcile, and you decide to end or change the relationship. During these times, it's tempting to point a finger, to blame yourself and others—but this is a futile exercise. Mark and Diane had had a particularly bitter break-up. Although they had tried to be friends afterward, they always ended up in an angry argument. Mark was about to write Diane off forever when he attended a workshop for divorced and separated couples. During the workshop, he realized he felt very guilty for not being with Diane. To make himself feel better, he created disagreements with her to prove he was right in not being with her. With this realization—and the realization that he truly loved her even though they were no longer together—Mark was able to tell Diane how much he cared for her, and accept the decision to not be together. They became friends—and haven't argued since.

The loss of a loved one—particularly through divorce or separation—is a wound that takes time to heal. Blame, anger, resentment, self-hate, all reinfect that wound. As Mark discovered, the healing process can be enhanced by accepting the loss without blame. Fortunately, more and more couples who separate are able to accept the break-up and actually do end up friends. Even though they decided not to remain life partners, they have genuine affection and respect for each other. Many of the people we spoke with counted ex-mates among their best friends. If a relationship is built on friendship, it is doubly sad to lose a best friend as well. And many couples are realizing they don't have to. Another thing we discovered: As painful and upsetting as breaking up can be, most of the people we spoke with admitted that in retrospect they saw the change was for the better.

You've built a relationship on a solid foundation of communication, mutuality, sharing, fun, and adventure. Of course, there's bound to be some disagreement and conflict. (Anyone looking for a relationship without any conflict at all had best stick to looking at pictures in *Playboy* or *Playgirl*.) But sustained and draining conflict—the kind that erodes relationships—is most often the result of a breakdown in one or more of the areas mentioned above. Like a building, a relationship requires maintenance and is subject to neglect. Here are some tips for the care and maintenance of relationships, to keep things running smoothly and trouble-free.

TIPS FOR LONG-TERM SUCCESS

1. Keep the lines of communication open. "Charles and I used to really enjoy going to baseball games together," Judy said. "At least that's what I thought. Then last year, he never even asked me. He'd just go with his buddies. I was enormously hurt, but I didn't say anything. I concluded there was something very wrong in our relationship, but I didn't know what. Then one day, I just blew up at him over nothing. In the course of this long, senseless argument, it finally came out that I was upset over the baseball thing. He looked shocked. 'I thought you were bored by baseball,' he said, 'so I figured I'd spare you.' Then it was my turn to be shocked. I guess since I'd never really told him how much fun I had going to games with him, he sort of assumed I wasn't interested."

When people are first getting to know one another, they are eager to communicate their dreams, values, likes, and dislikes. They want to learn everything they can about each other. However, after several months or several years, they drift into the "danger zone" and think they know all they need to know about the other person. Instead of finding out, they rely on mind reading and assumption. They get so lazy that the only exercise they get is jumping to conclusions. The result is damaging miscommunications like the one between Judy and Charles. You need an ongoing, regularly scheduled process for clearing up all communications, miscommunications, and noncommunications. Be sure to include:

- Things I meant to say but didn't.
- Things I didn't mean to say but did.
- Things I especially like about you.

Be sure to end anything that can be construed as criticism with genuine positive appreciation. Remember the "3 for 1 rule"— three positives for every negative.

2. Communicate responsibly. There's a Paul Simon song where he tells his lover he appreciates her telling it like it is, but asks for "a little tenderness with your honesty." People sometimes mistake "honesty" for carelessly dumping their anger, judgments, distress on another person who is supposed to be able to take it because "he/she loves me." There is no faster way to erode positive feelings than by making the relationship a dumping ground for negative ones. Not that anger or negative feelings should be withheld;

but we should be aware of the effect our way of expressing those feelings has on our partner. "Jane and I were on this endless merry-go-round," Greg says. "She would complain, and I would get angry about her complaining, and she would start crying. This would make me angrier. With the help of a counselor, we were finally able to see what we were doing to each other. She learned how much her complaining upset me, and I learned how sensitive she was to my anger. We developed these signals that either of us could give that meant, 'Please back off.' We'd deescalate, and it was a lot easier to get to the real issues." When problems are aired and handled quickly, you prevent the build-up of resentment that can erode rapport.

3. **Move from the problem frame to the solution frame.** One of the most troublesome patterns in long-term relationships is "collecting garbage"—that is, looking for things the other person is doing wrong and then dredging up things that were wrong in the past. When that happens, every argument is an old argument. And because the past really cannot be changed, there is never a solution. So we recommend that instead of asking, "Why did you do that?" or "What are YOU going to do to make me feel better?" you ask, "What can WE do to work this out?" This puts you both on the same side looking "out there" at the problem instead of staring each other down as adversaries. Keep the focus on what you want rather than on what you don't want. If there's any doubt in your mind, ask the other person: What is it you really want? How would you like it to be? Then go for what you both want and enjoy.

4. **Look for mutually satisfying solutions.** There are three main frames for solving conflict—the "win-lose" model, the "lose-lose" model, and the "win-win" model. The "win-lose" model is the traditional power-based, authoritarian method—one person gets his way, the other doesn't. Traditionally, men have called the shots and women have followed. Or women have given men the impression they were going along—but they called the shots. We don't think either of these "all or none" models works very well, because when the person with the most physical and psychological power dominates, the other person is devalued. Her contribution to the relationship becomes limited. And she often ends up cynical and resentful. "I've spoiled relationships by doing things I didn't want to do," Margaret says. "I just didn't know how to stand up to the other person, or felt guilty about making a fuss. But at the same time, I just withdrew myself and stopped trusting."

The "lose-lose" model, better known as "compromise,"

is an attempt to create mutuality by taking something away from each partner. To illustrate the limits of compromise, let's say that George and Martha are planning a vacation. George wants to go to New York, Martha wants to visit California. Both are unyielding in their position. Finally, they agree to compromise on a middle point—and they end up going to Kansas. In this model, neither George nor Martha really won anything. Instead of trying to come to a mutually satisfying solution, they created mutuality by arriving at a mutually dissatisfying one.

Fortunately, there is another model. The "win-win" model—or successful negotiation—involves identifying the needs of both partners and coming up with a solution that fits both persons' needs. As it turns out, George's need was not really to go to New York, nor was Martha's need to go to California. After discussing their real needs and desires, they discovered that George was interested in pursuing his hobby, archaeology, by visiting museums. Martha just wanted to be someplace sunny. Once they realized that, they were able to do some research and found several very interesting archaeological sites in Southern California. George became even more excited about visiting the actual sites than he was about the museums; and Martha was more than glad to accompany him anywhere that was sunny.

We recommend going for the "win-win," "yours-mine-ours" frame right away instead of insisting on having your own way or settling for something that isn't what either of you wants. Sometimes you will find that the solution you come up with is actually BETTER than what either of you thought possible. Betty and Dan had decided to move in together, and they chose Betty's apartment because it was larger. Unfortunately, they disagreed about where to place their furniture. "We ended up moving the furniture into four different configurations," Dan says, "to see how we liked it. We eliminated two right away, which left us firmly opposed. Betty wanted it one way, I wanted it the other. We were too tired to argue anymore, so I suggested going out to dinner. Over dinner, we realized we needed a place that was large enough to encompass both our styles. We became really excited about that possibility, and three weeks later we found just the right place, where I can have my space and she can have hers."

5. Don't neglect fun and adventure. The most powerful form of positive reinforcement for your relationship is to share fun and adventure. Fun is the fuel that kindles caring and rapport. Often in the pressure of everyday life, we forget that relationships need

care just as we do. Too often, we let the problems take over our time and energy. If you find yourself asking, "Where did the fun go?" try this little game. Go out for dinner or for a walk or just out on the porch and play "Remember when we used to _____?" Each person takes a turn filling in the blank. When you have a list of "used tos," choose the ones you want to do the most and schedule them again. Do this every week—until you're creating new good times. So that when you play "Remember when we used to _____?" twenty years from now, you'll be able to remember the things you're doing today.

6. **Agree to disagree agreeably.** No two people—not even Siamese twins—are likely to agree on everything. We recommend that you stretch yourself to encompass disagreements, differences in style, differences in opinion—unless you find a particular difference nonnegotiable. Says Linda, "My boyfriend and I had a conflict over a political issue, and it became really ridiculous. We argued about it constantly. Finally, he said to me, 'Look, does this issue really affect our relationship?' I thought about it and realized that it had absolutely no bearing on what we did together or how we did it. We laughed and agreed that we had already discussed it as much as we needed to, and that we never had to talk about it again. And we haven't."

7. **Maintain your social activities network.** It is all too common for people to couple up, then go "underground." While it can be fun and very important to a new relationship to spend a lot of time together, couples sometimes forget they have friends out there, and how to have fun with others. As a result, they tend to depend on each other for things best provided by other friends and acquaintances. For some couples, "togetherness" means depriving themselves of activities their mates don't enjoy. For others, it means engaging in activities whether they enjoy them or not. We keep hearing that it's more important to spend high-quality time together than to spend high-quantity time together. As the fast-food company says, "You deserve a break today." So does your partner. Be sure you kindle the warmth of old friendships—and create new ones—as you build your relationship with your partner.

A FINAL WORD . . .

We hope you have enjoyed your journey with us and have begun to use the material we've presented to create more joy, friendship, and intimacy in your life. Remember that meeting people and building relationships is a lifetime process that needs to be practiced. We hope the stories and ideas in this book have kindled a fire in you to meet the people you want to meet and create the bonds of friendship. There are many more fascinating people and exciting experiences ahead of you in your life journey. Now, go out there and find them!

We'd love to hear your success stories and the fun ways you've met new friends. Write to us care of Writer's Digest Books, 9933 Alliance Road, Cincinnati, Ohio 45242.

INDEX

Get More Out of Life!
... these books show you how

Clutter's Last Stand, by Don Aslett. In this "ultimate self-improvement book," Aslett gives you the courage to sift, sort, and toss whatever is detrimental to your housekeeping (and mental!) health—and get rid of clutter once and for all. 276 pages/$9.95, paperback

Is There Life After Housework?, by Don Aslett. America's #1 Cleaning Expert shows you how to save up to 75% of the time you now spend cleaning your home by using the tools and techniques the professionals use. 178 pages/$8.95, paperback

Do I Dust or Vacuum First?, by Don Aslett. Here are answers to the 100 most-often-asked housecleaning questions, including how to keep your no-wax floors looking like new and how to clean brick walls. 183 pages/$7.95, paperback

It's Here ... Somewhere!, by Alice Fulton and Pauline Hatch. The authors show you how to get more places out of your spaces with their *room-by-room* approach to getting your home in order. They take you step by step through every drawer, closet, and corner of your house, helping you decide what to keep and how and where to store it. 192 pages/$8.95, paperback

Guilt-Proof Parenting: How to Be a Better Parent Through Those Tough Teen Years, by Priscilla de Garcia & Robert Wolenik. Learn how to put any parental guilt aside and determine the *real* causes of your teens' problems. A practical, caring guide. 216 pages/$15.95

How to Get Organized When You Don't Have the Time, by Stephanie Culp. A simple, 5-step approach to organization that will fit even the busiest schedule. 216 pages/$10.95, paperback

Available at bookstores, or order direct from the publisher by calling TOLL-FREE 1-800-543-4644 (In Ohio 1-800-551-0884). Or send the cost of the book, plus $2.50 postage and handling for one book, 50¢ for each additional book, to:
Writer's Digest Books
1507 Dana Avenue
Cincinnati, OH 45207

(Prices subject to change without notice.)